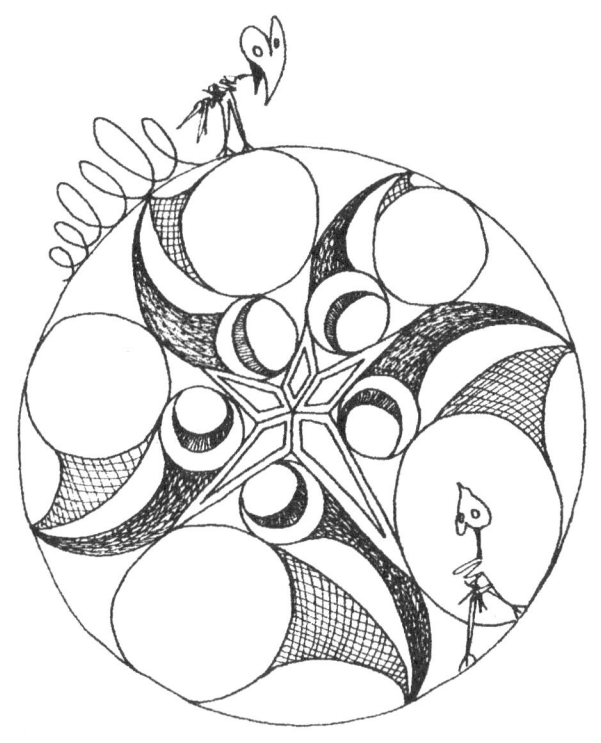

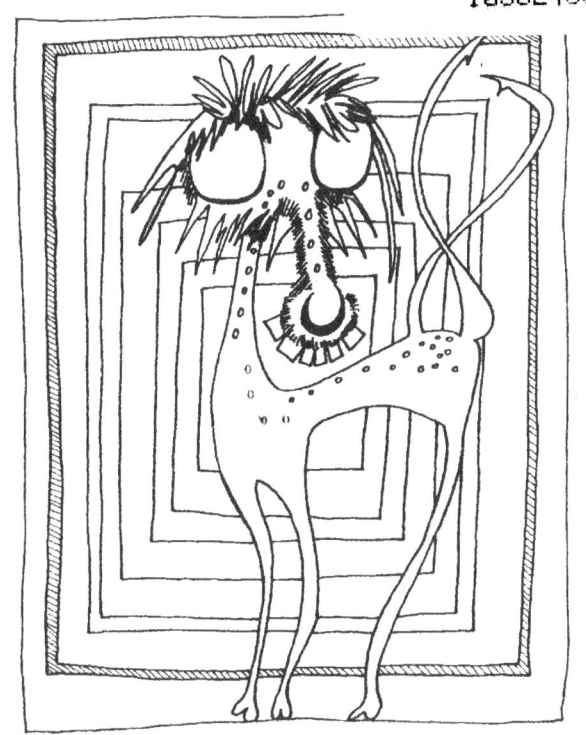

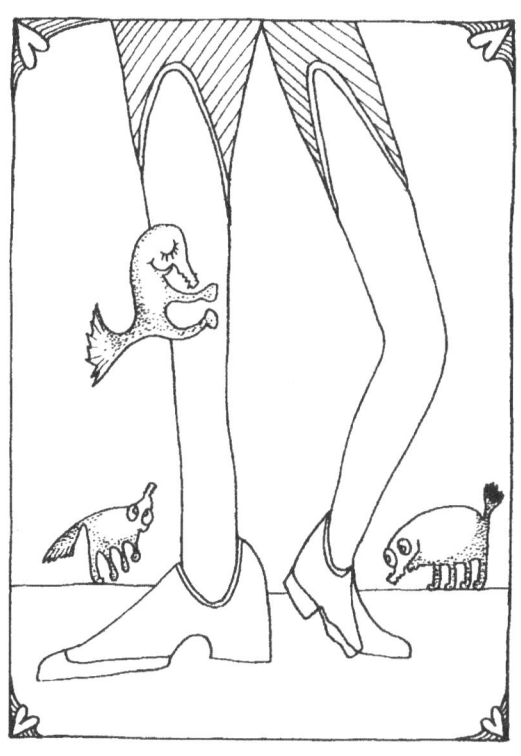

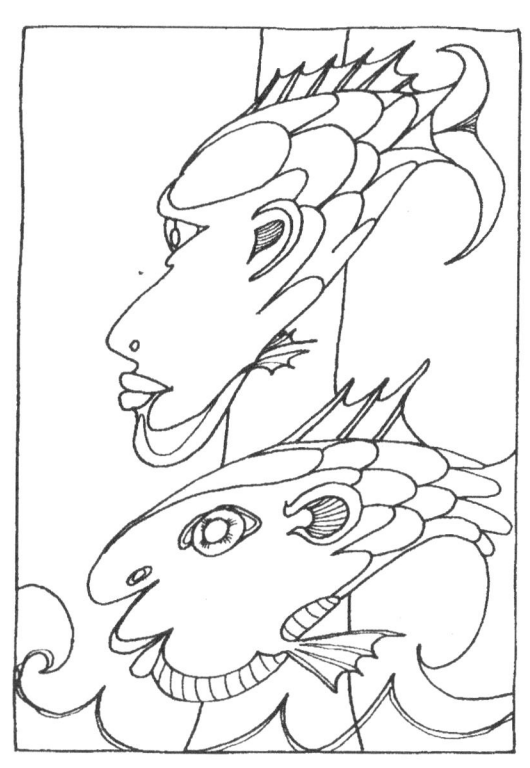

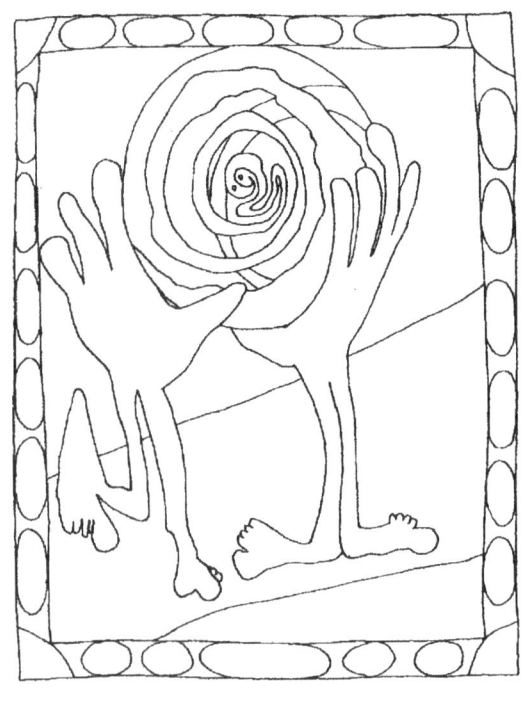
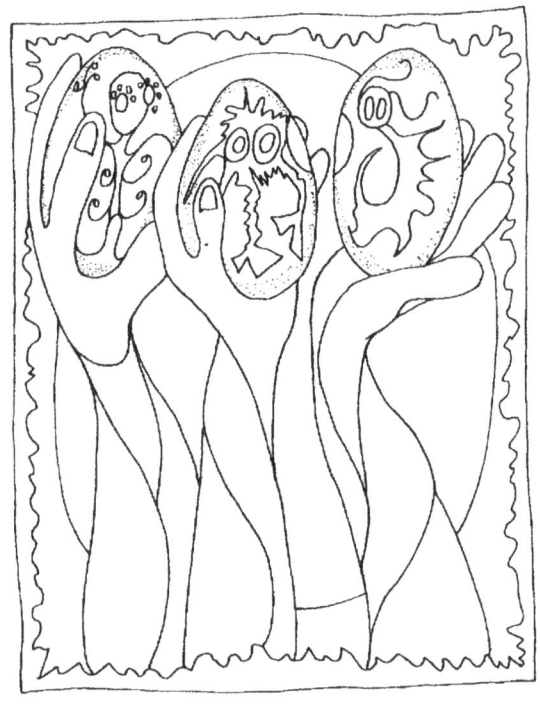
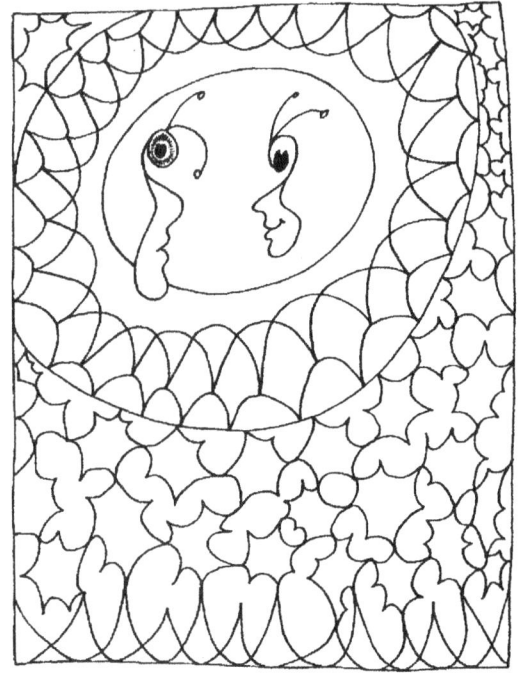
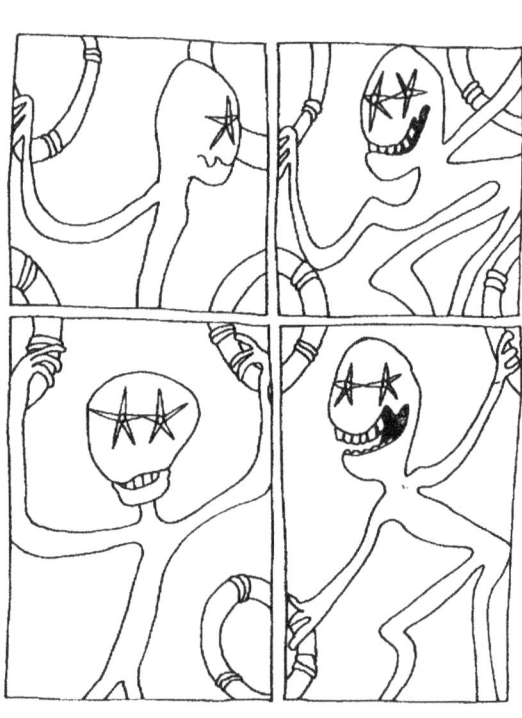

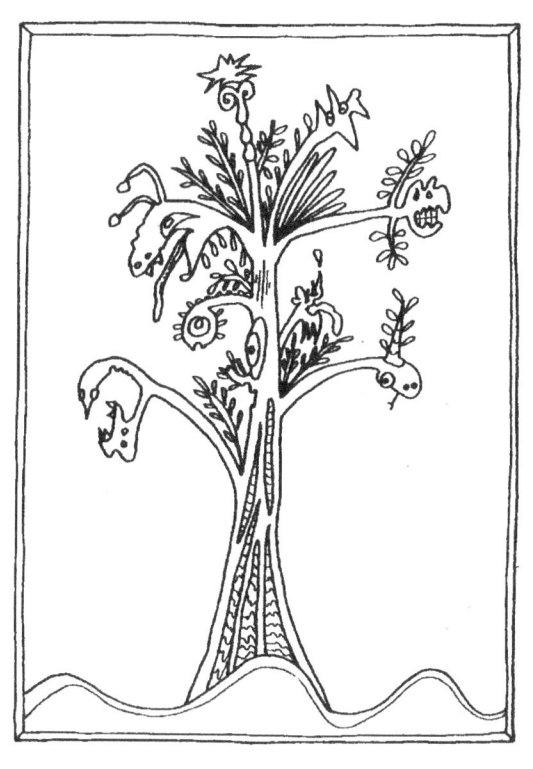

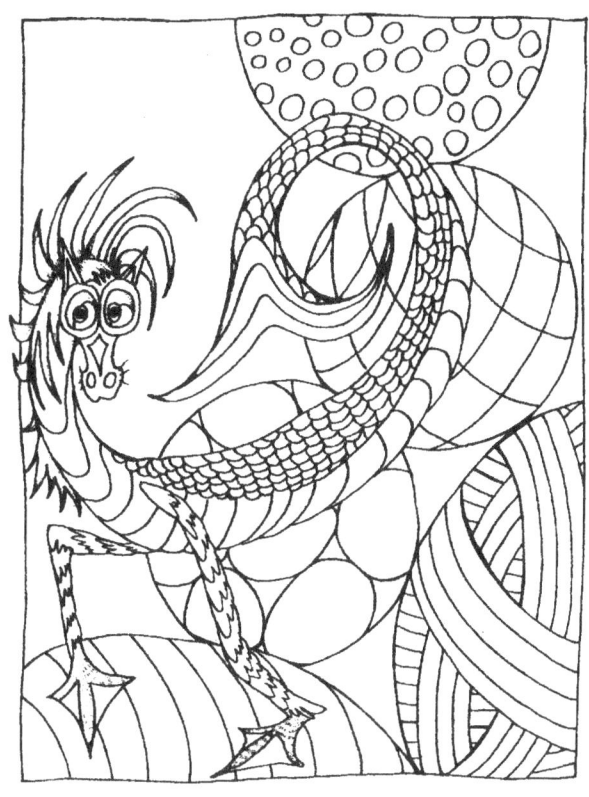

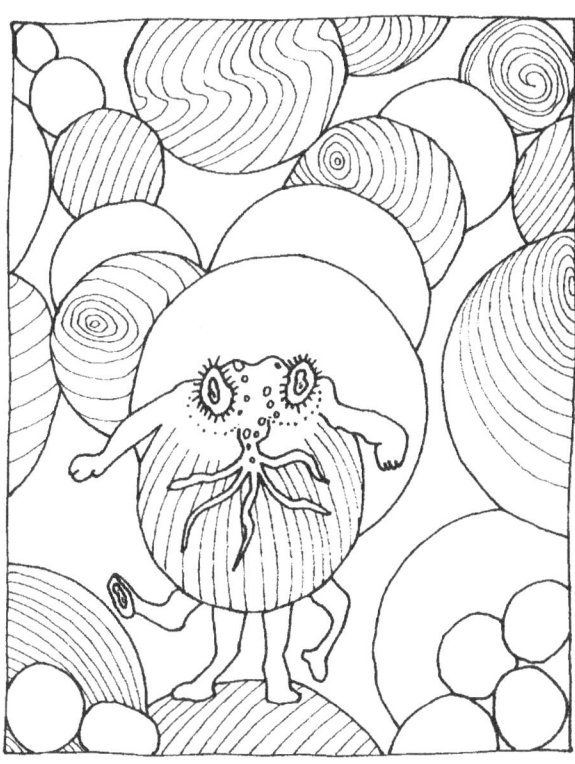

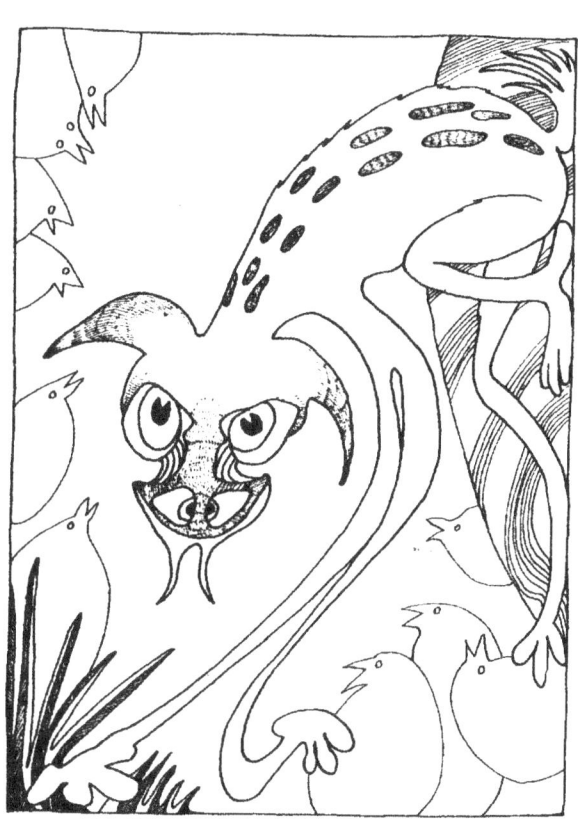

CREATURA - 2

70 Drawings by Joan Worth

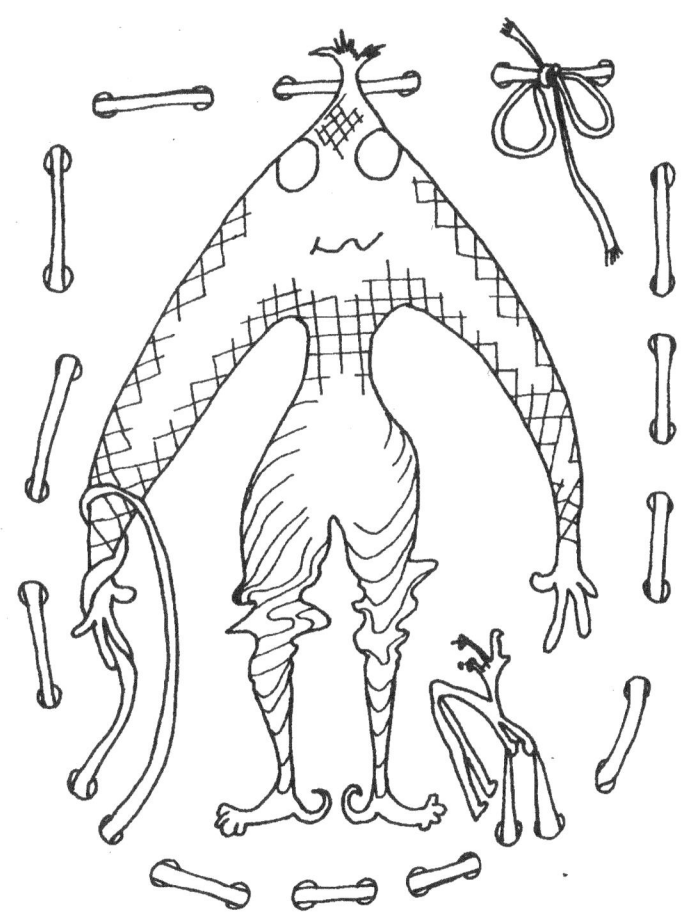

ISBN-13: 978-1545497029
ISBN-10: 1545497028

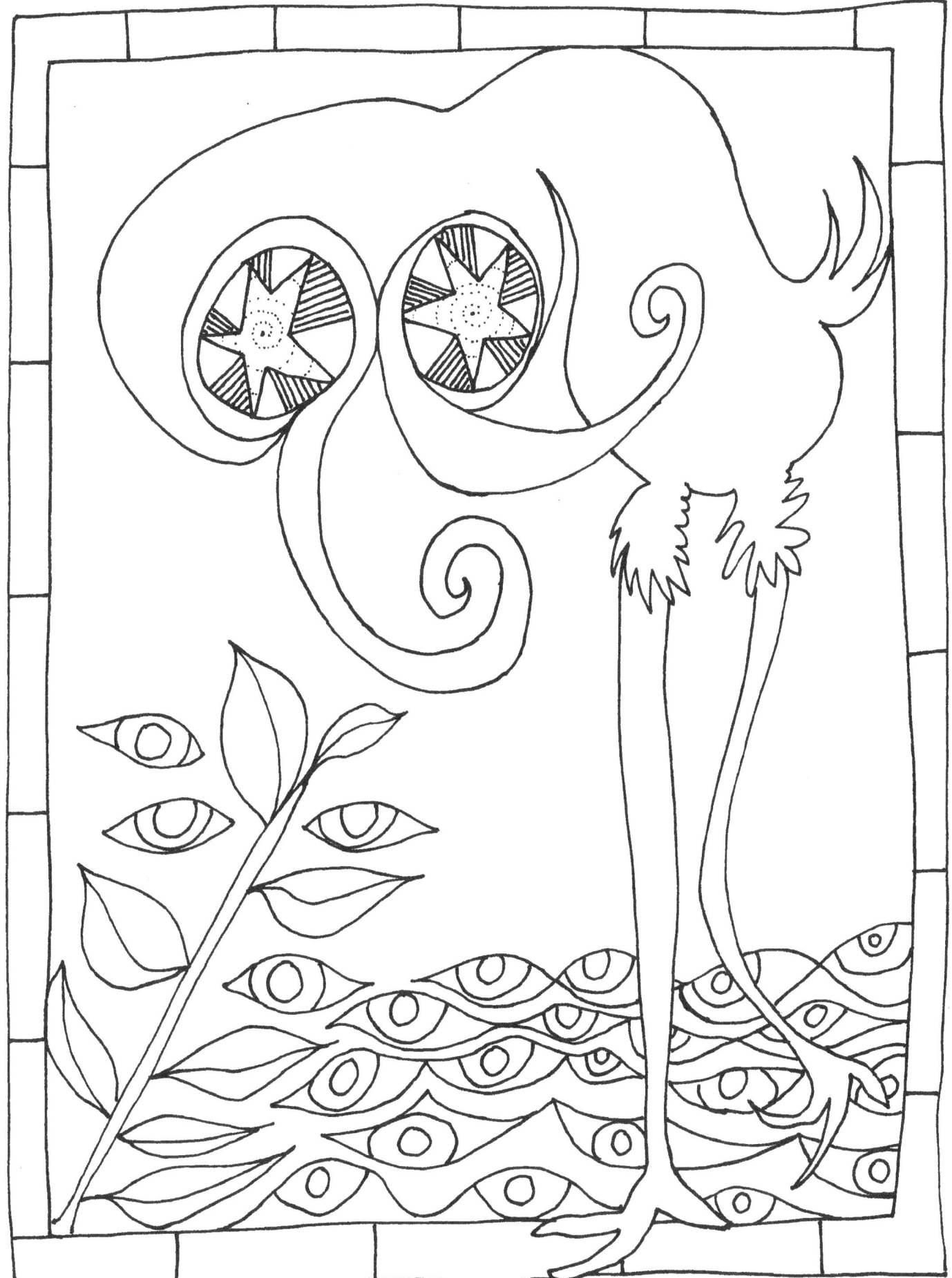

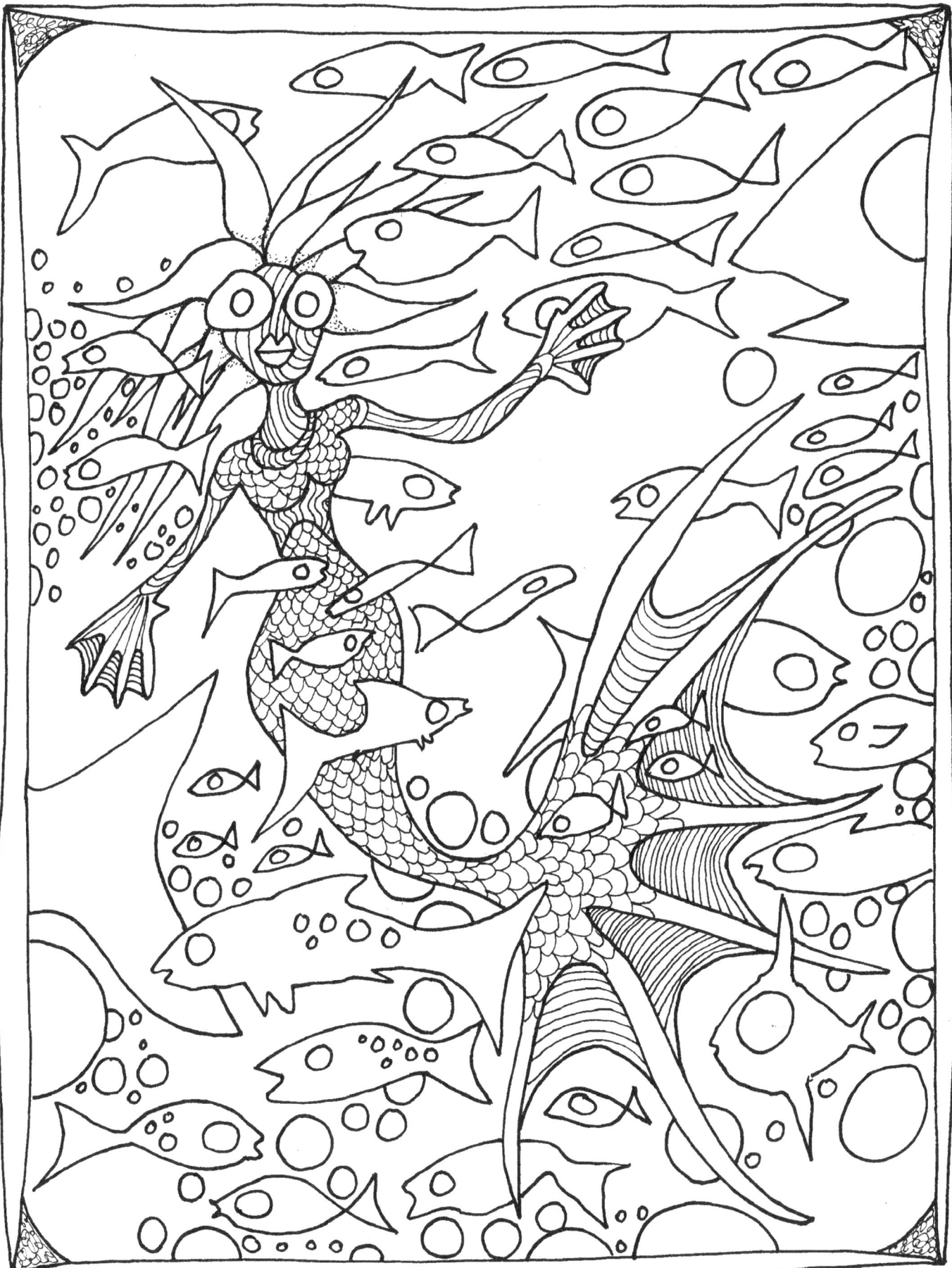

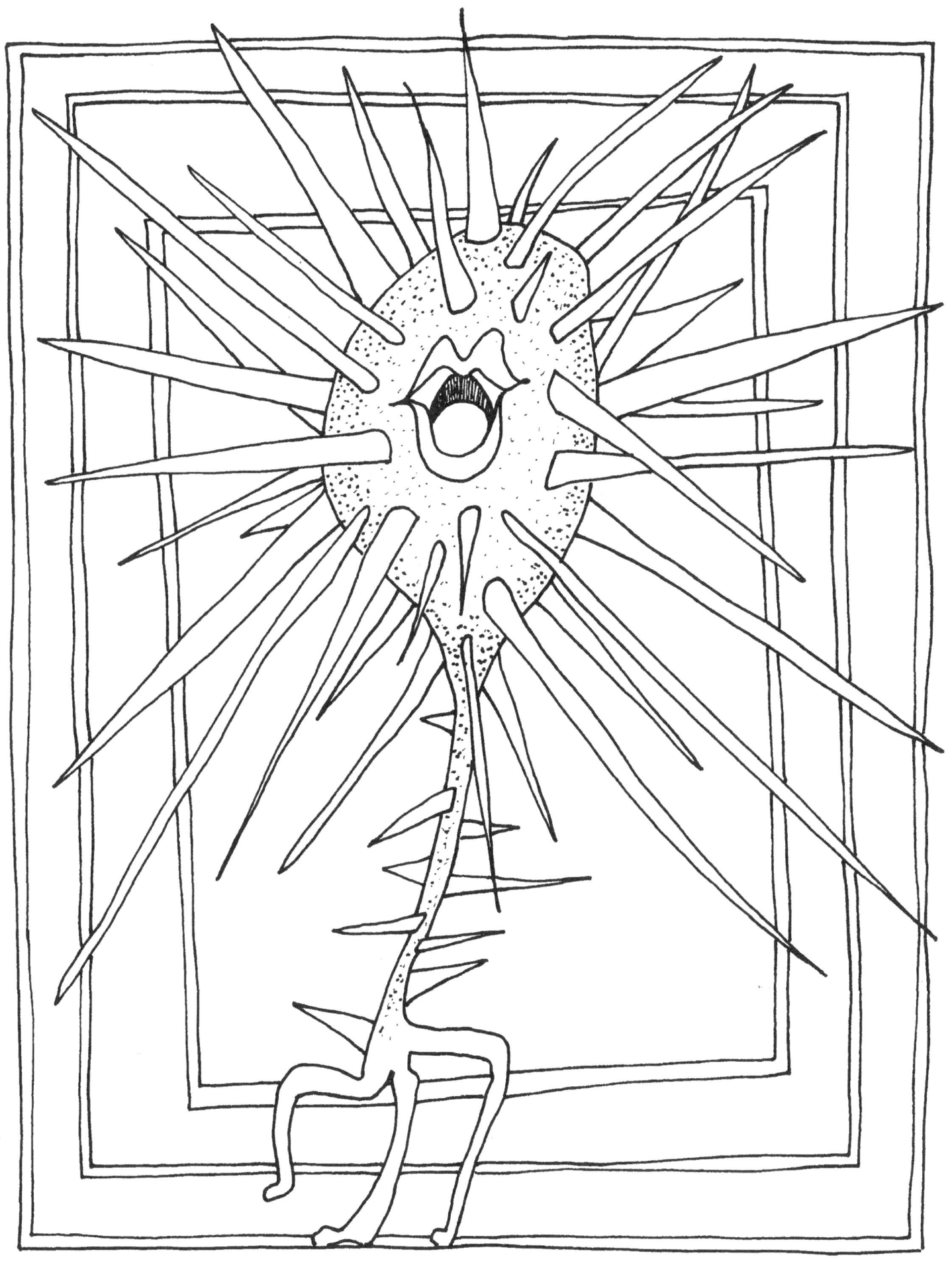

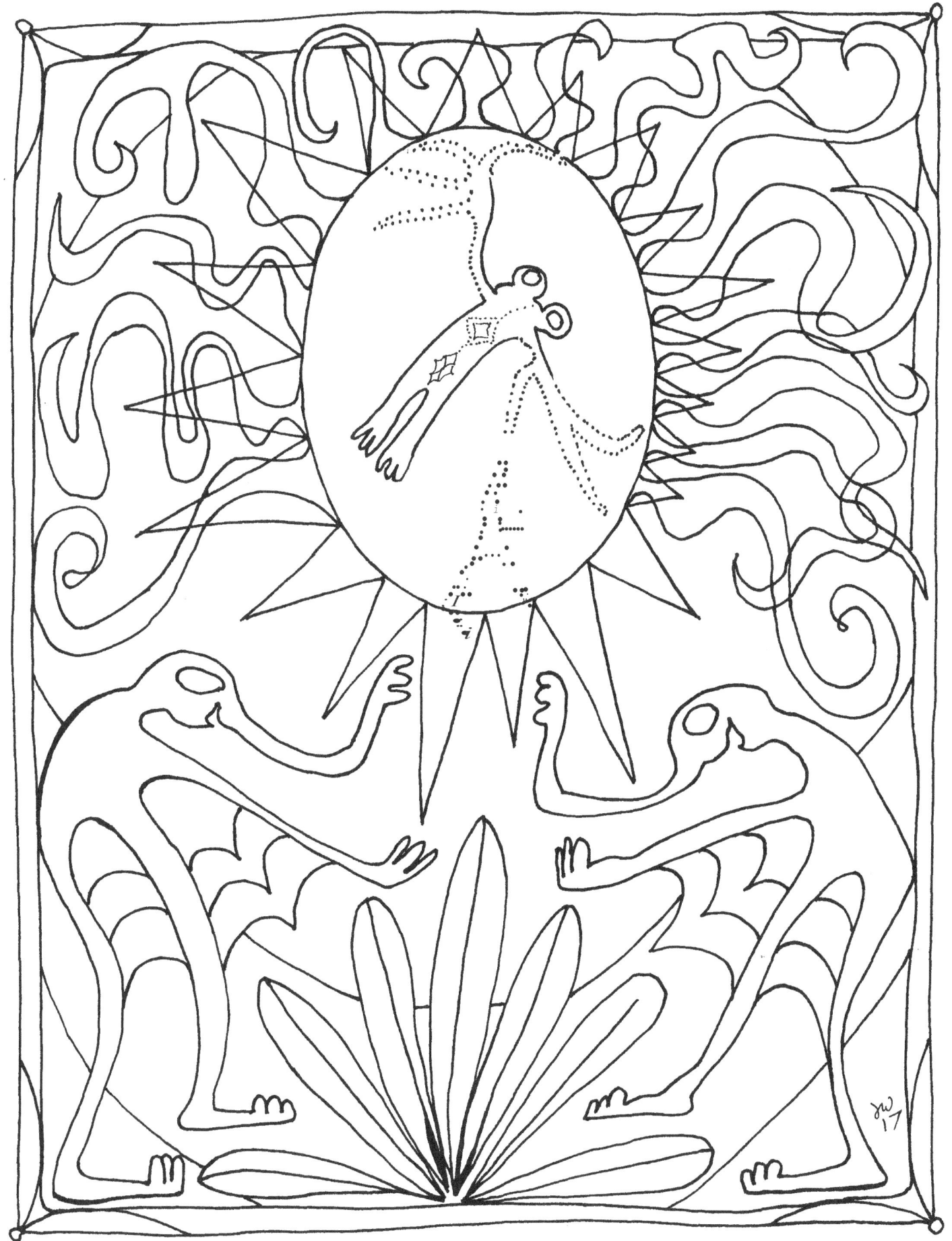

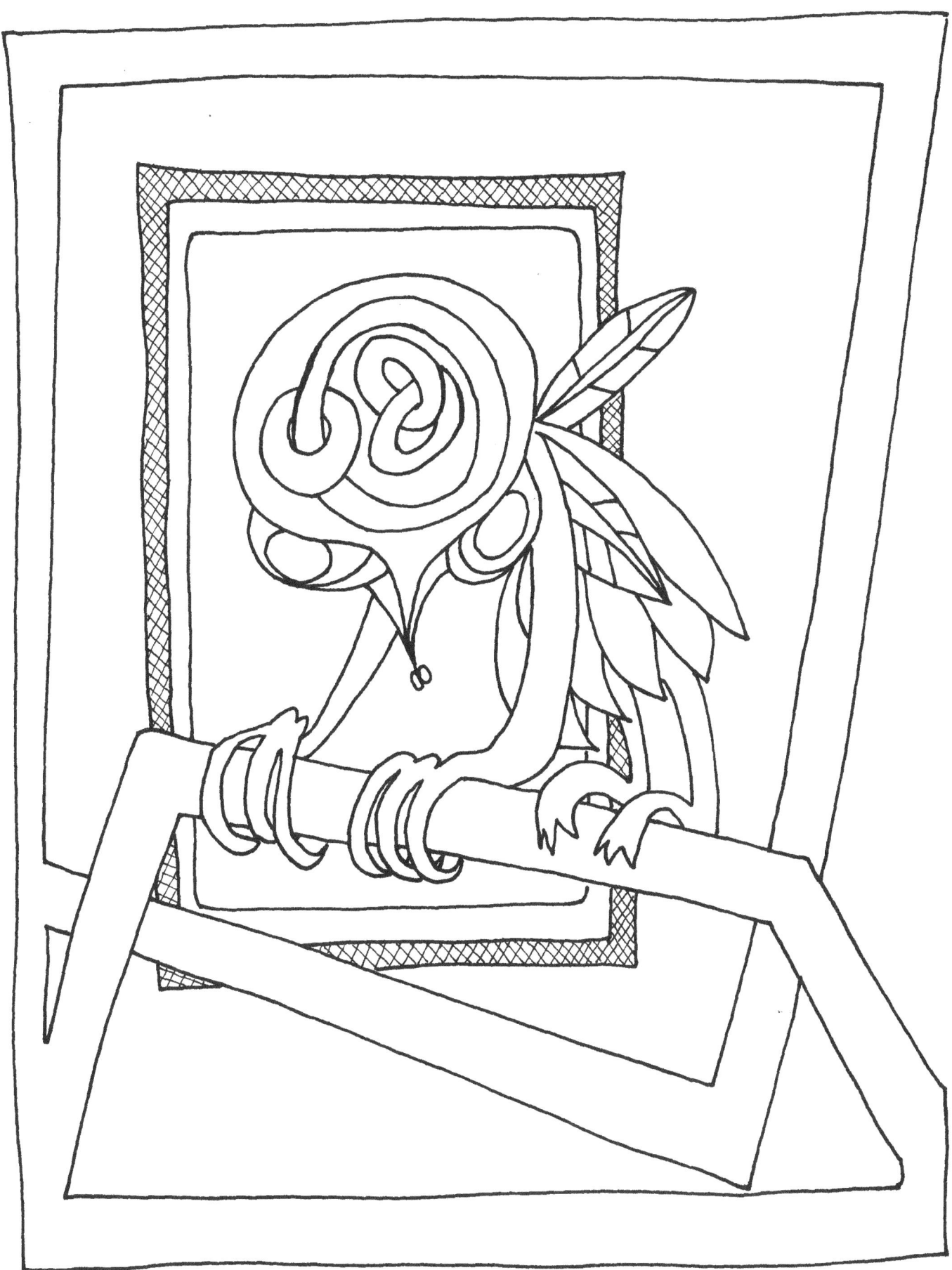

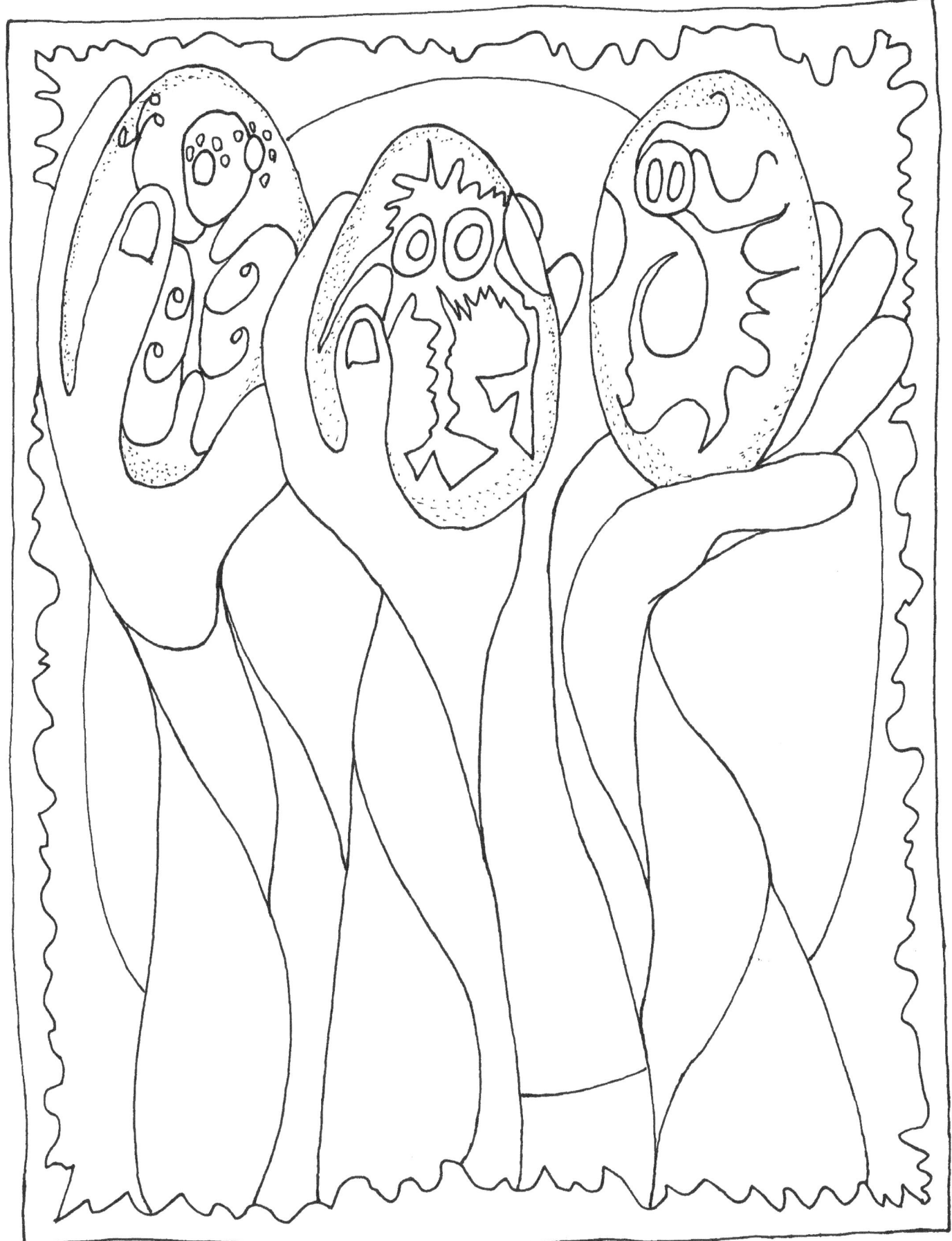

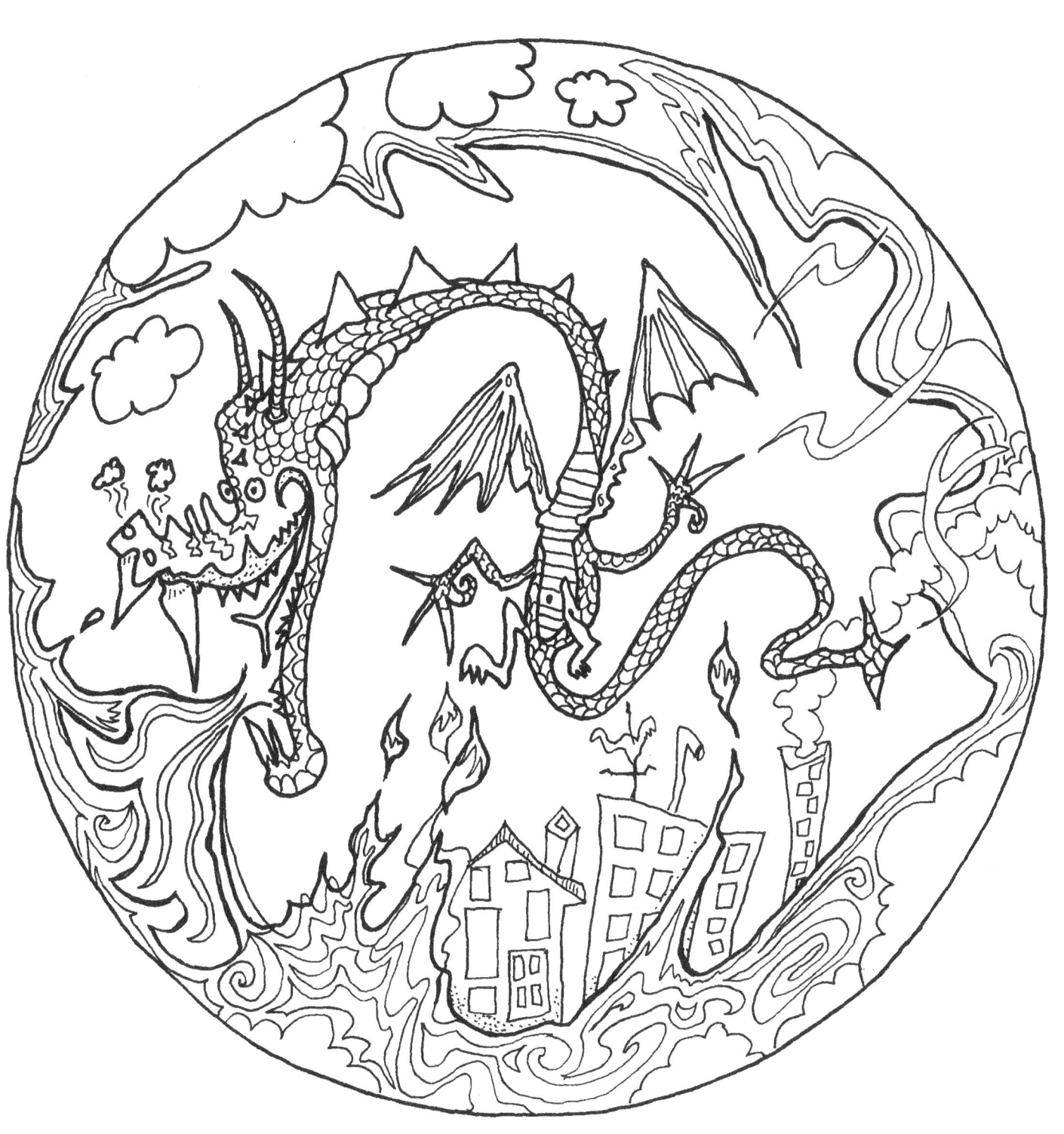

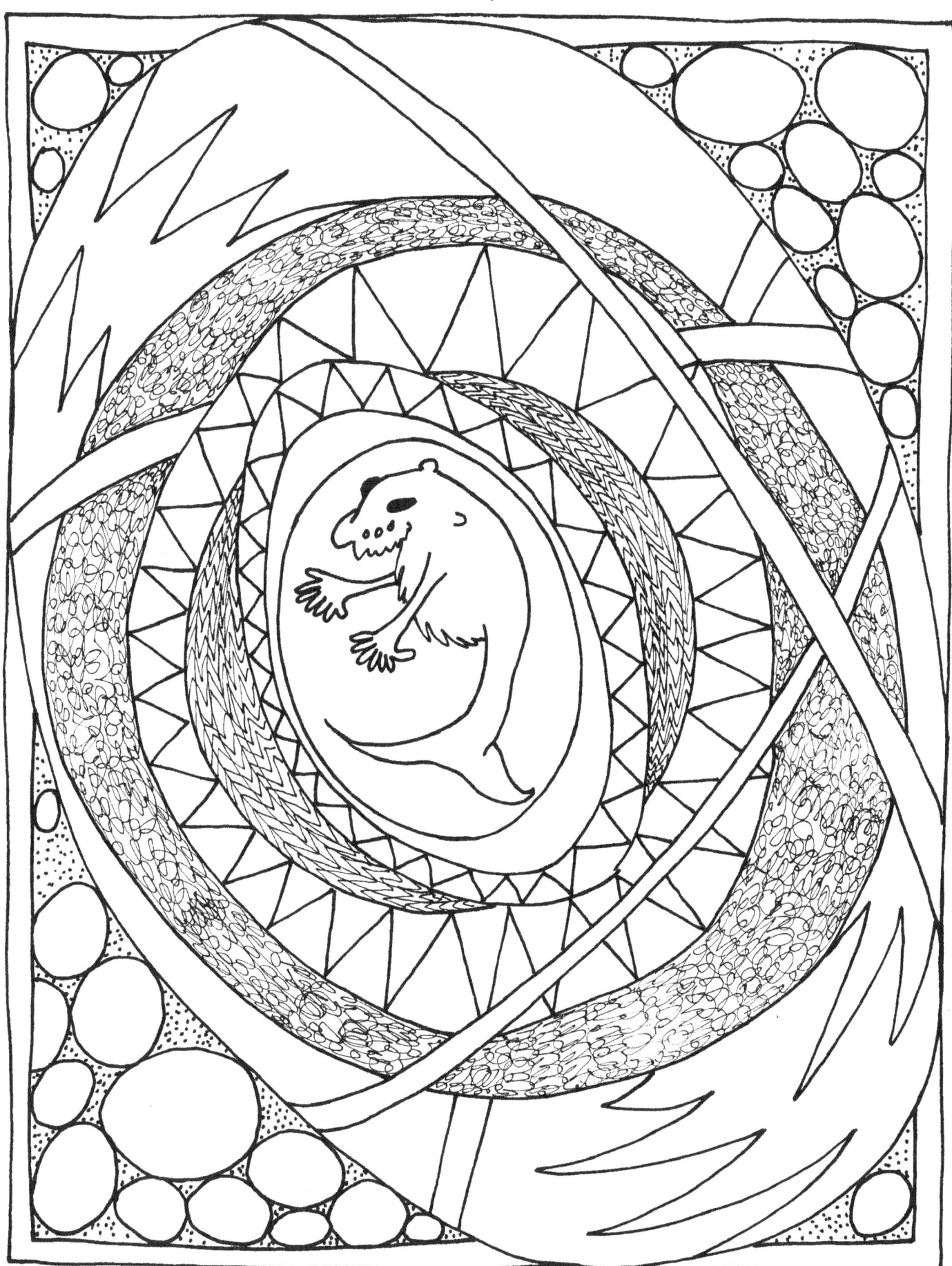

Creatura 2 - ©2017 Joan Worth

.

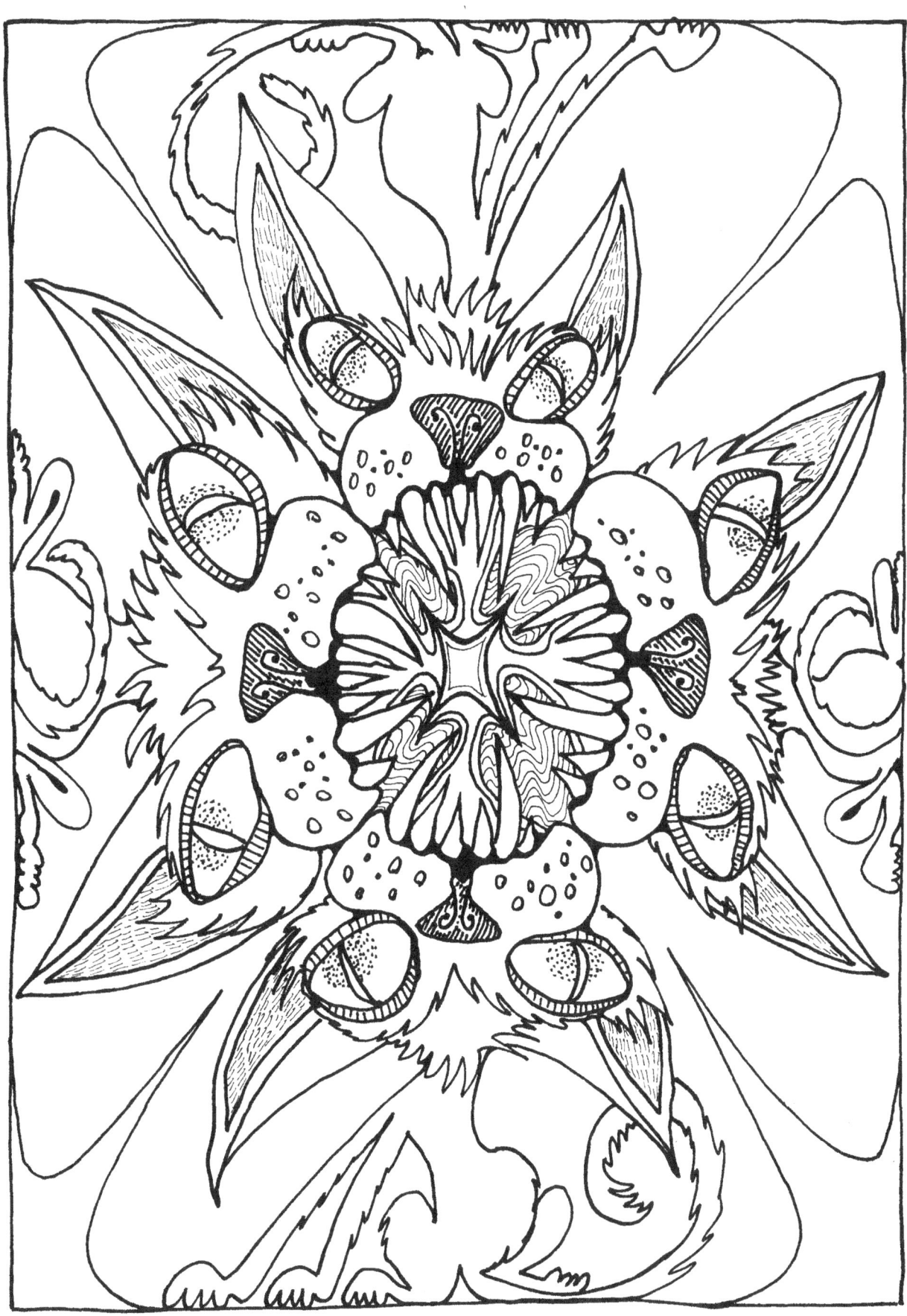

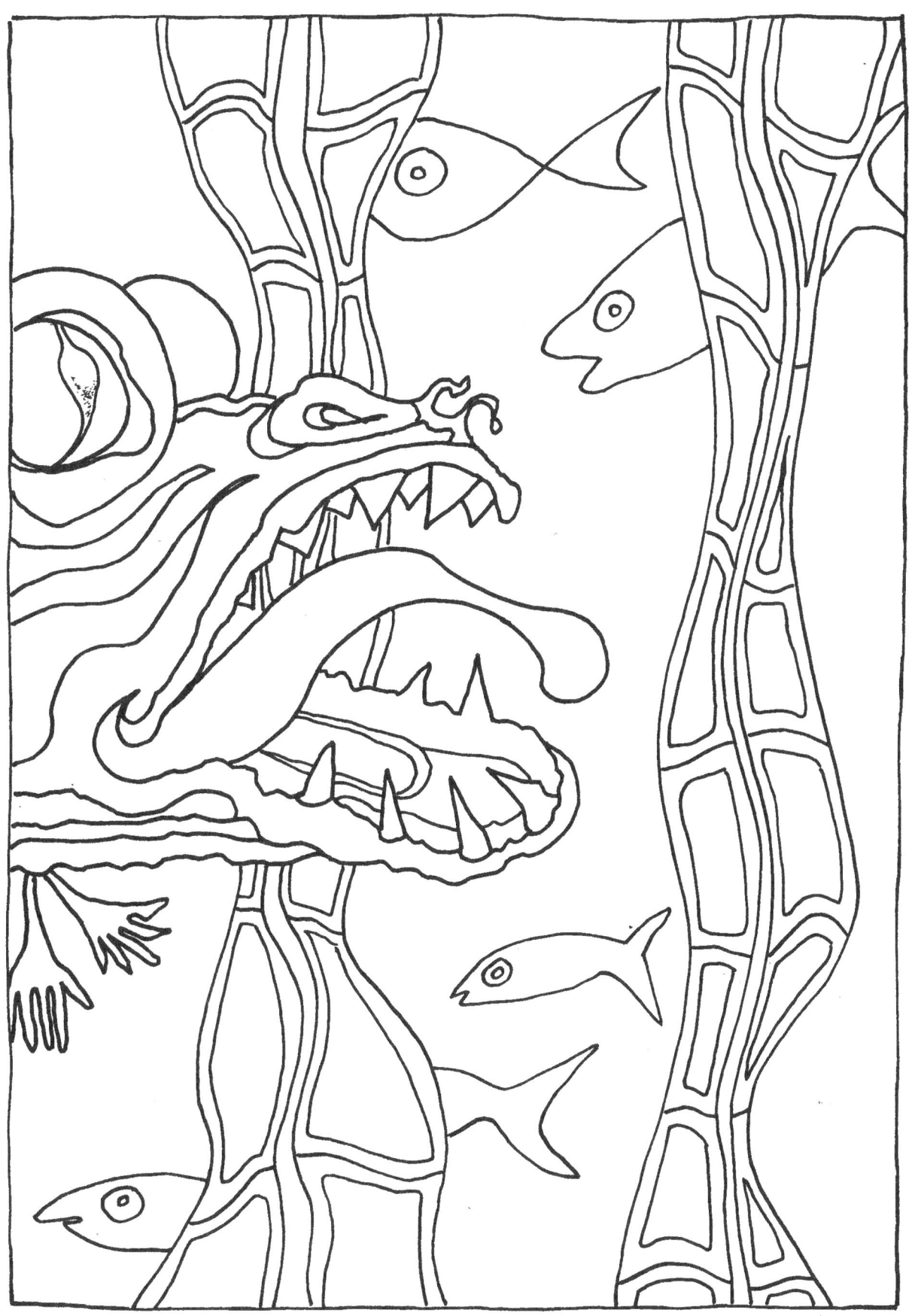

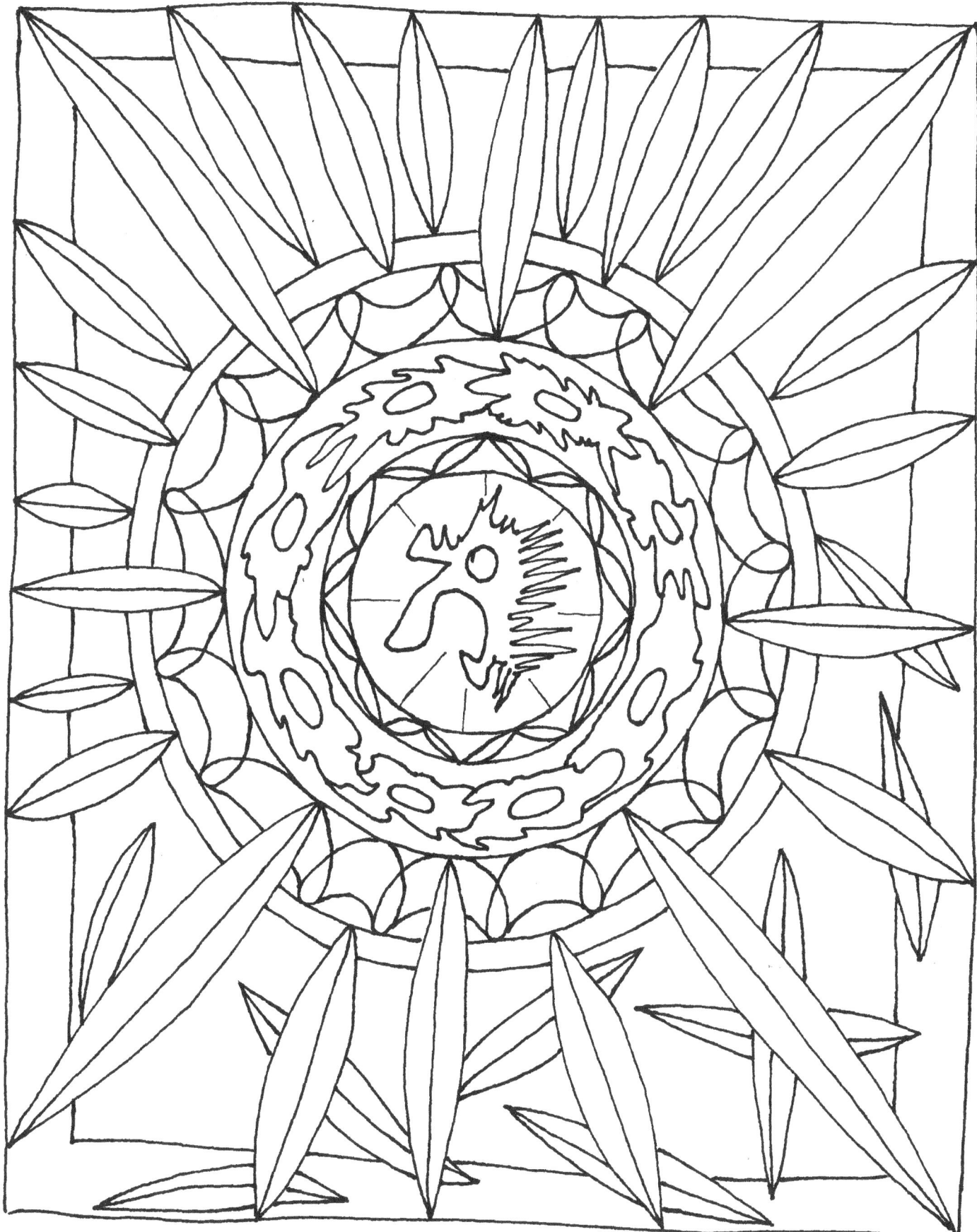

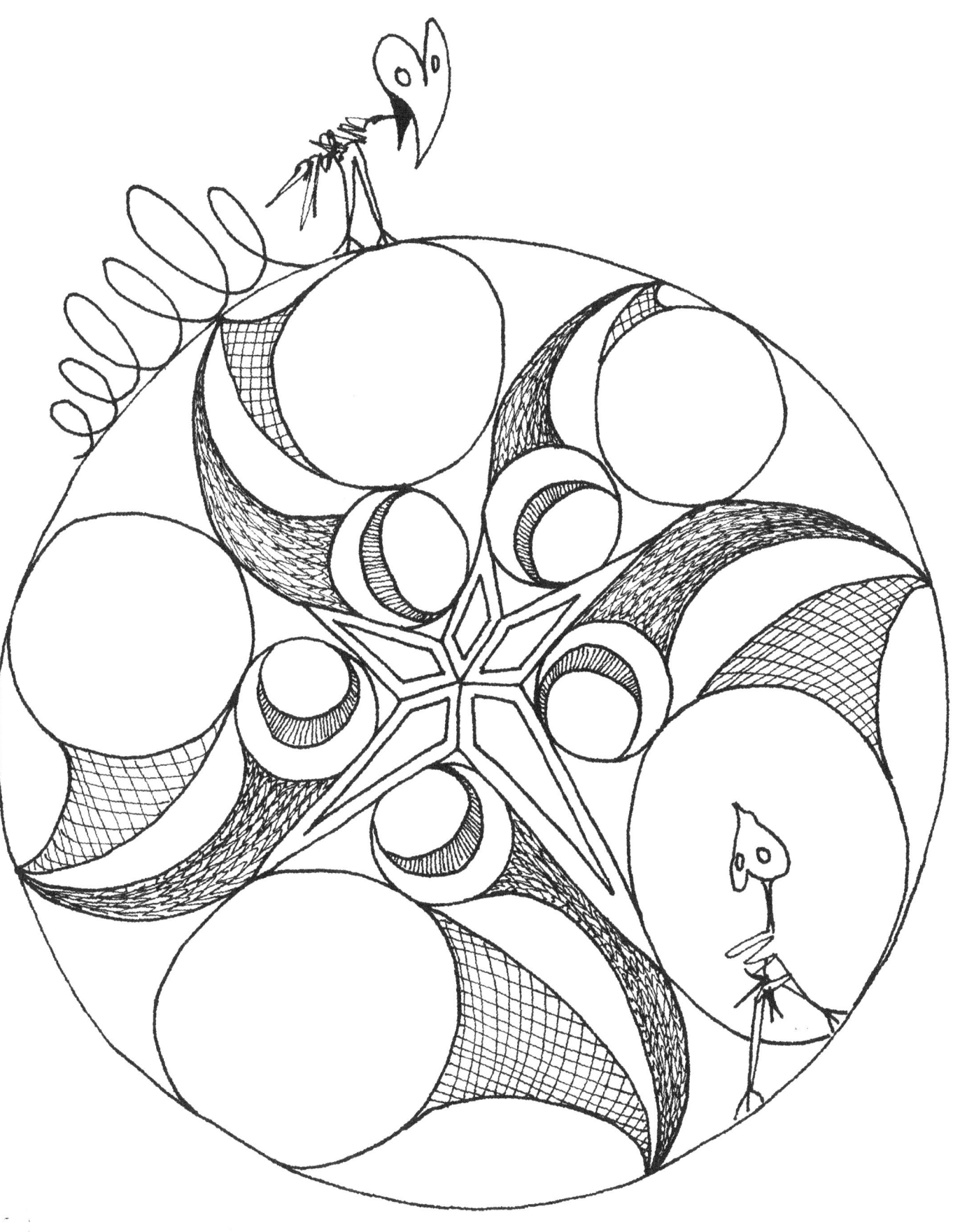

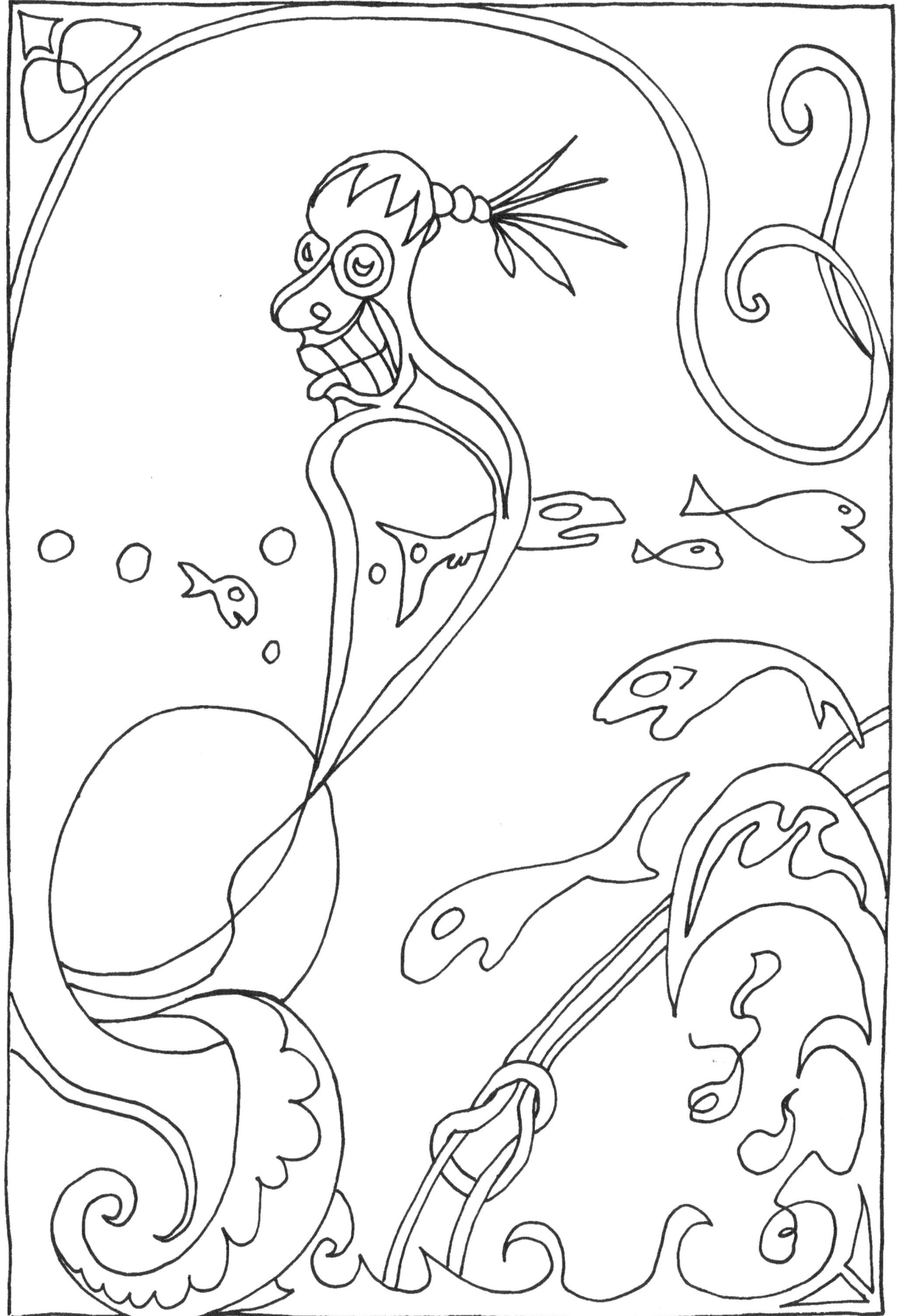

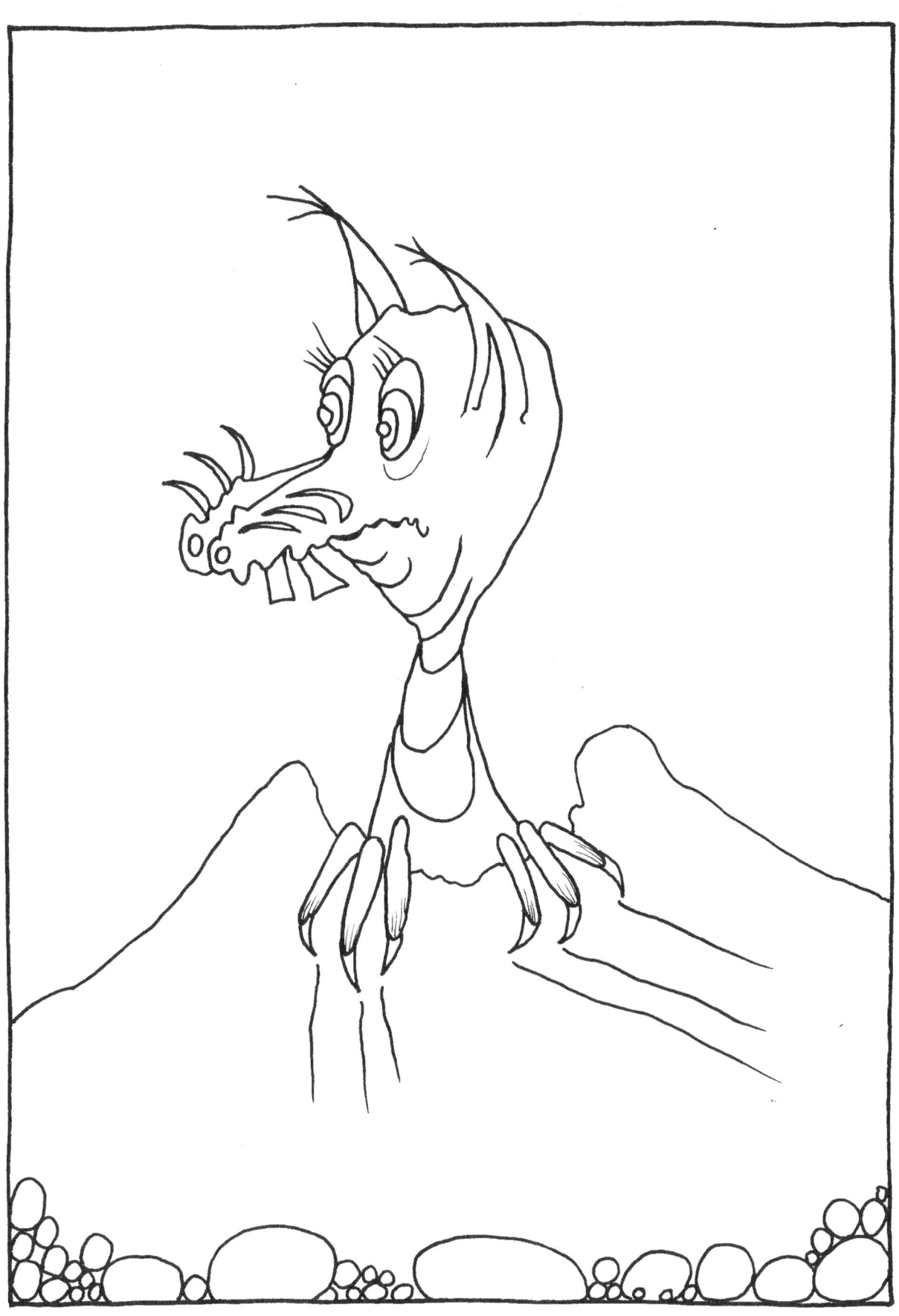

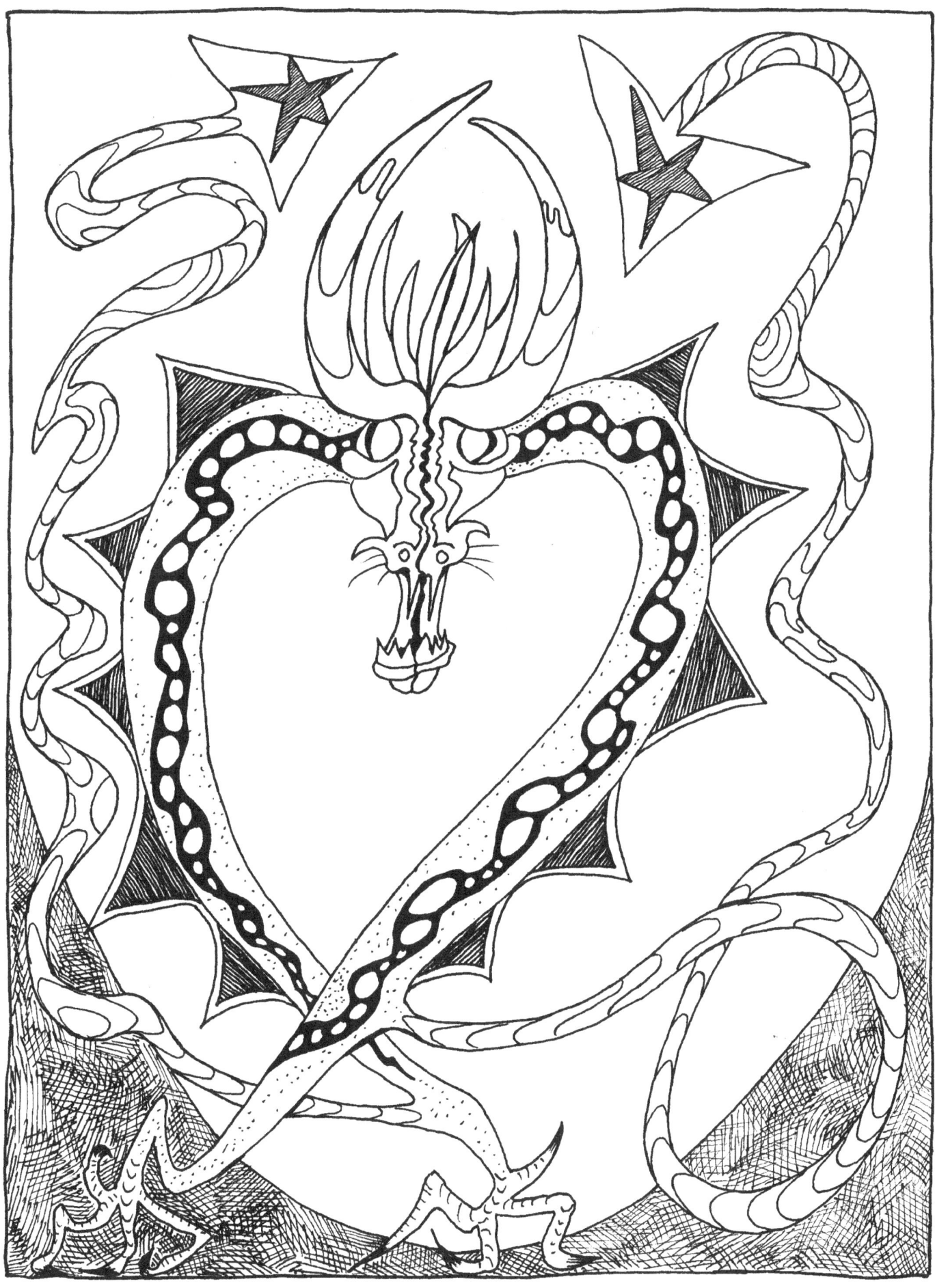

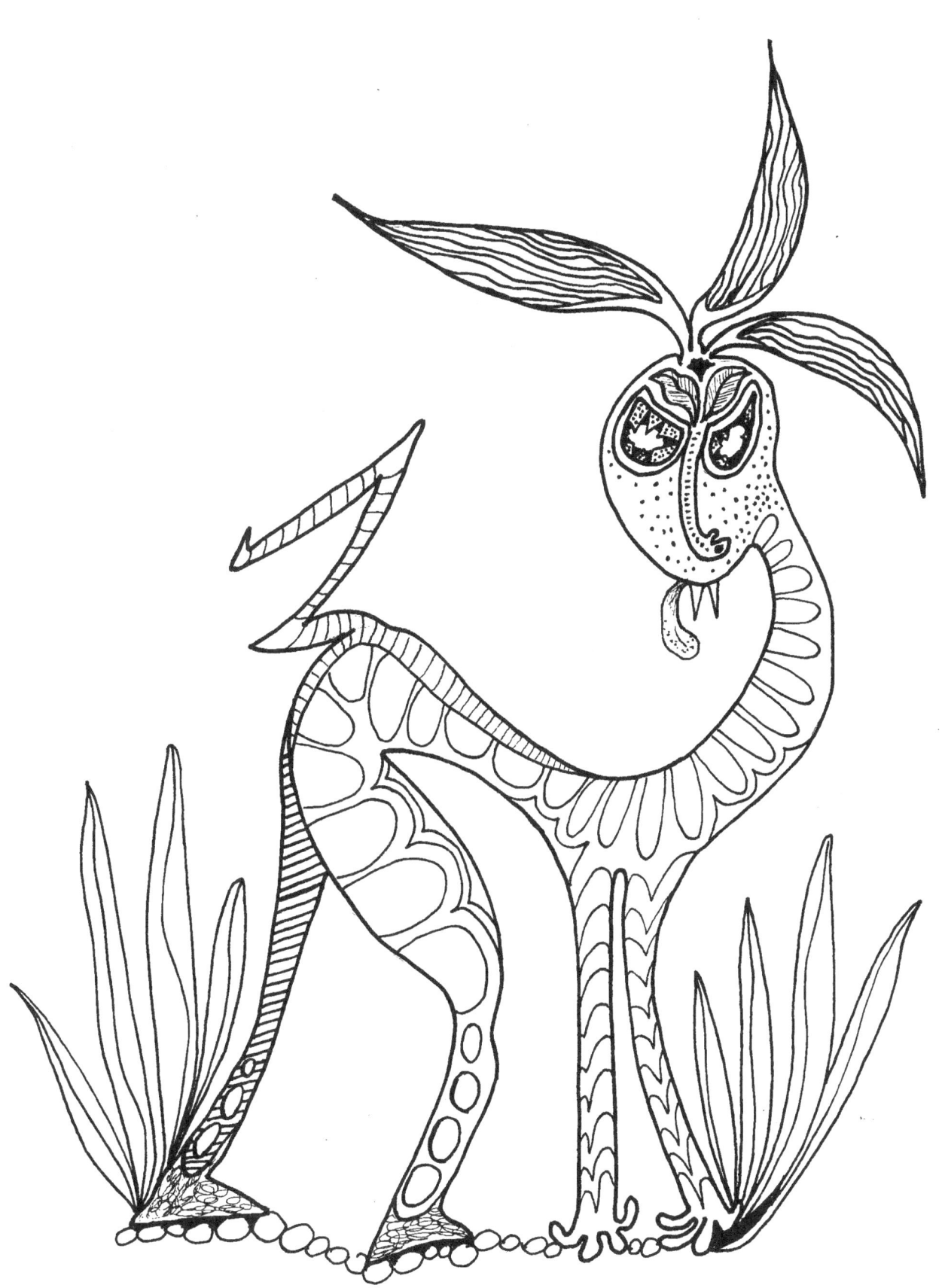

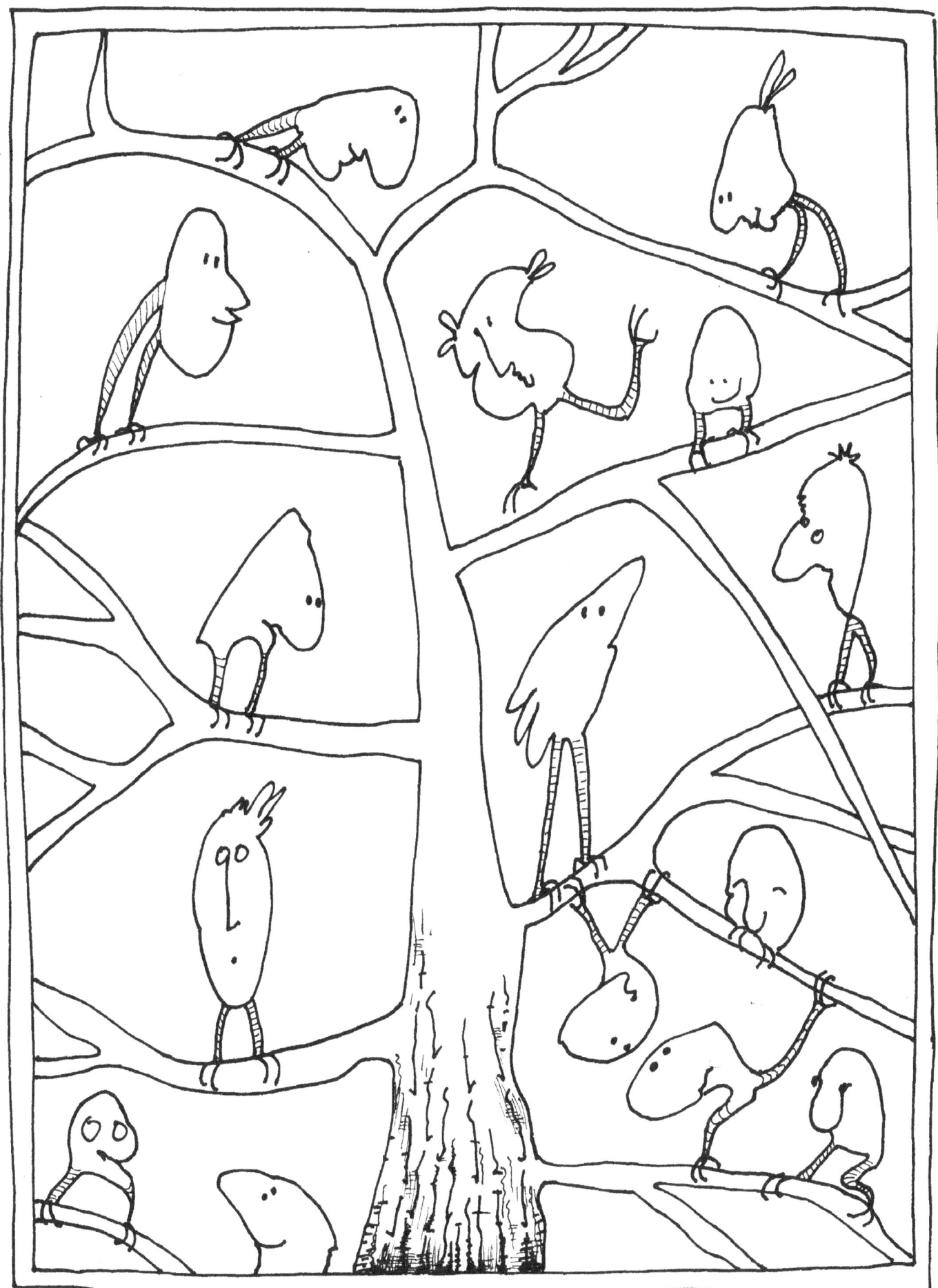

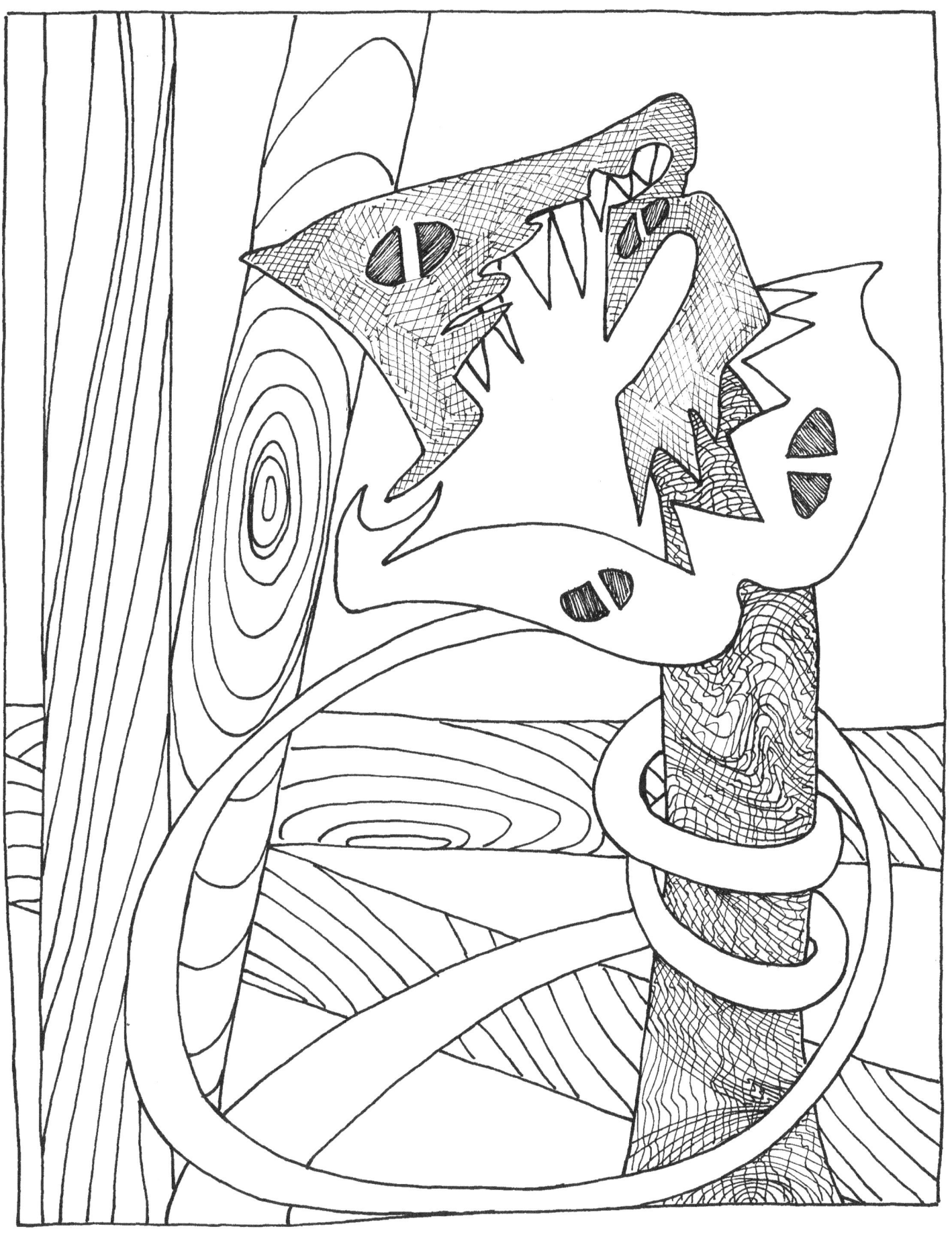

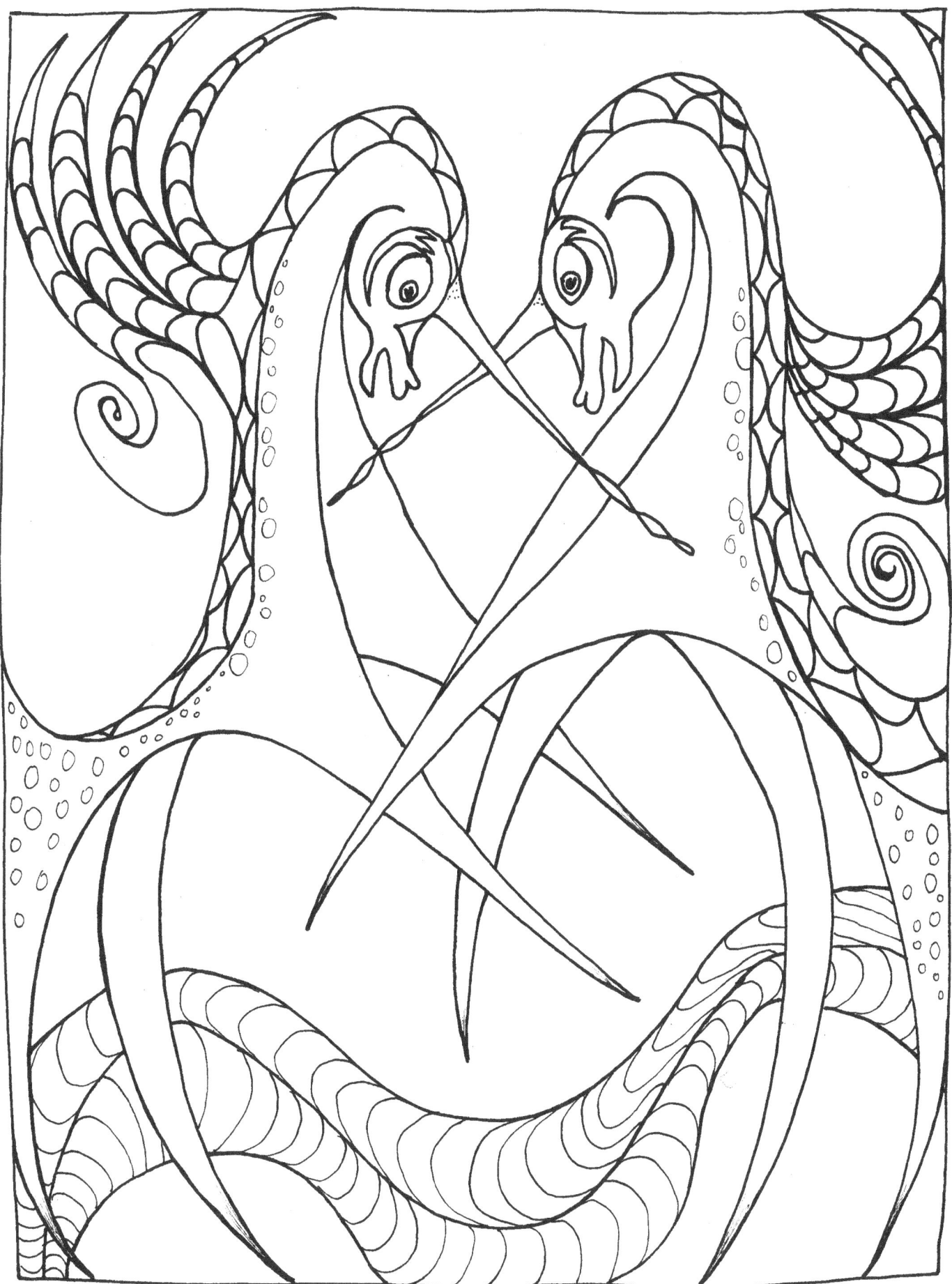

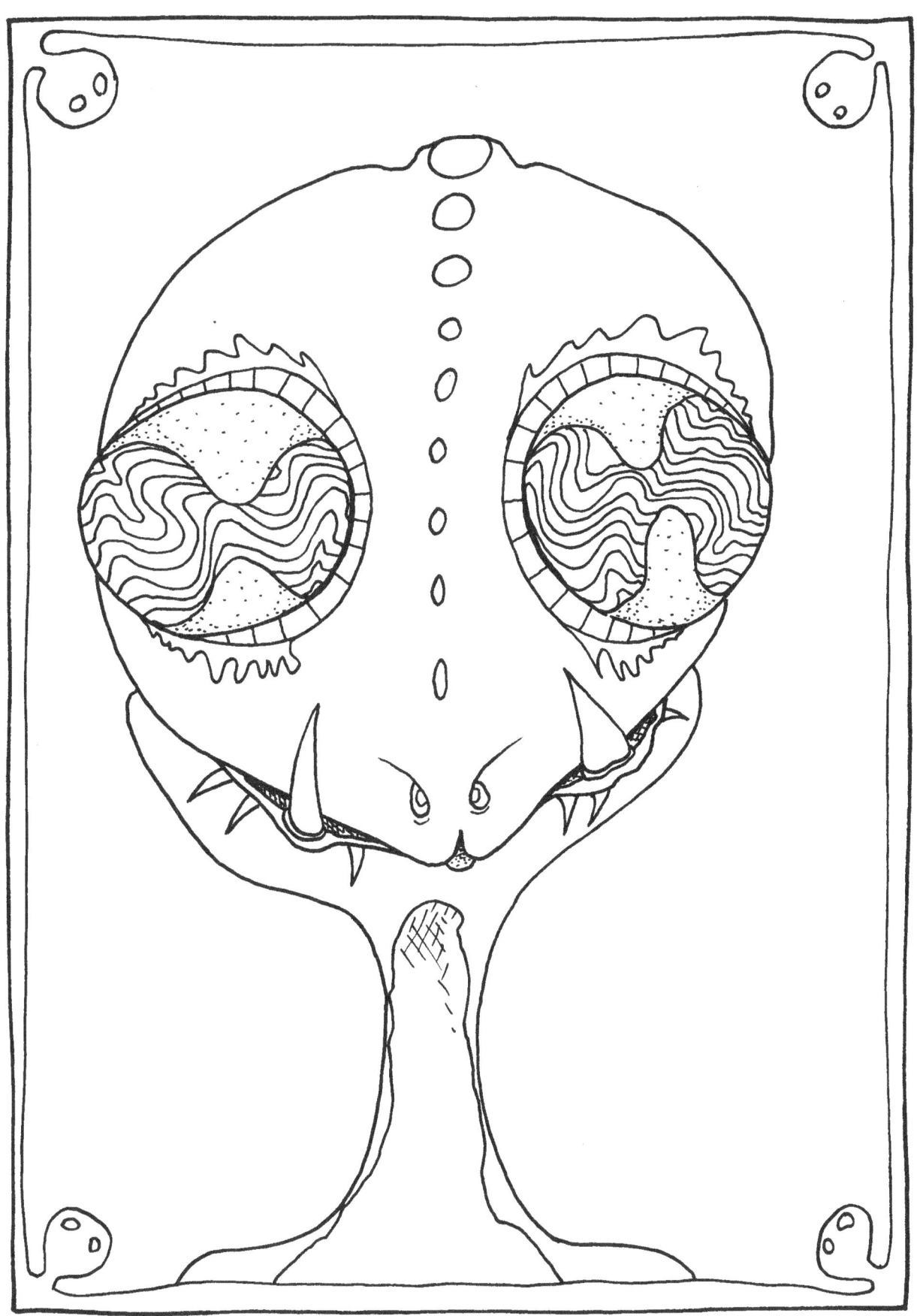

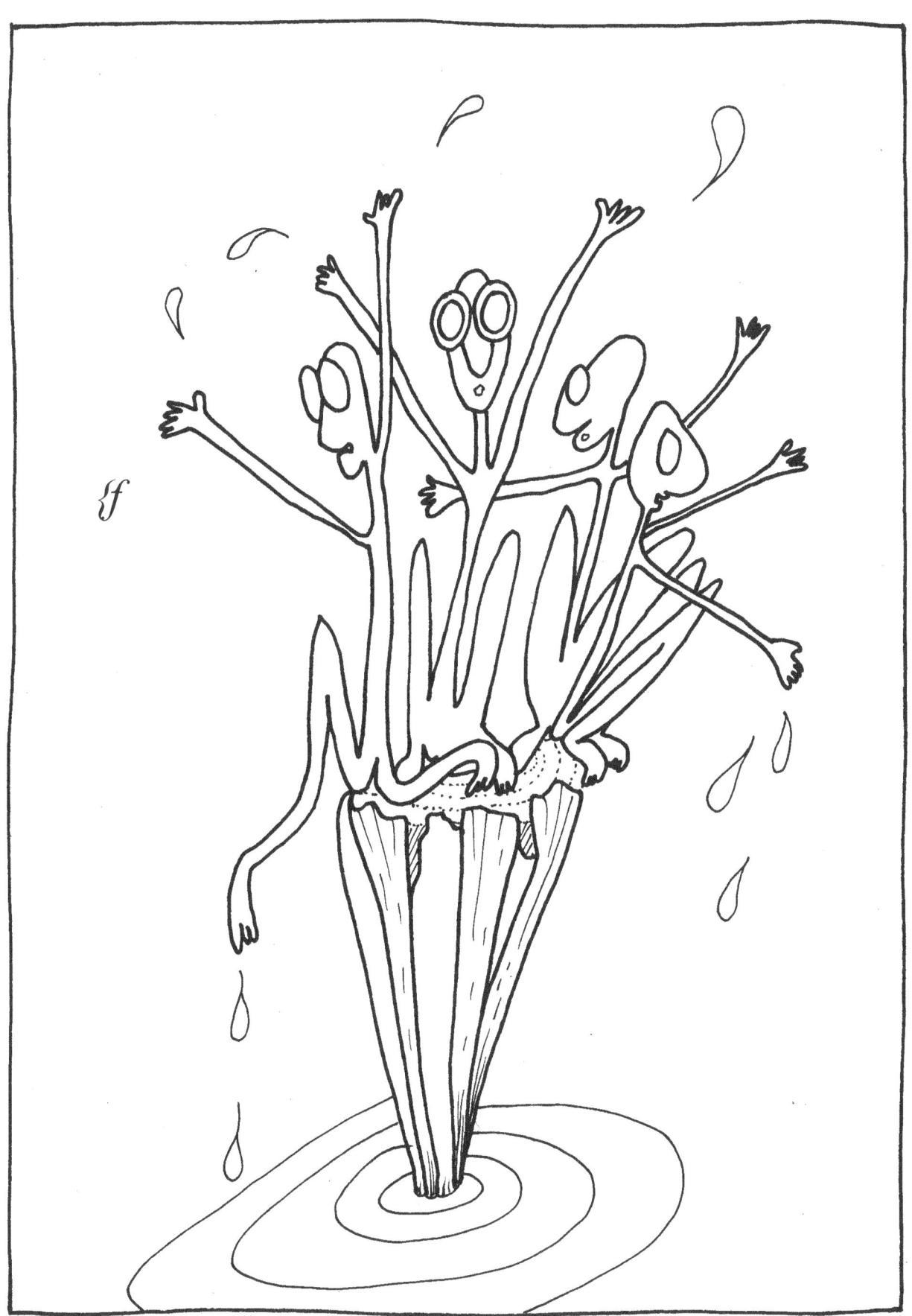

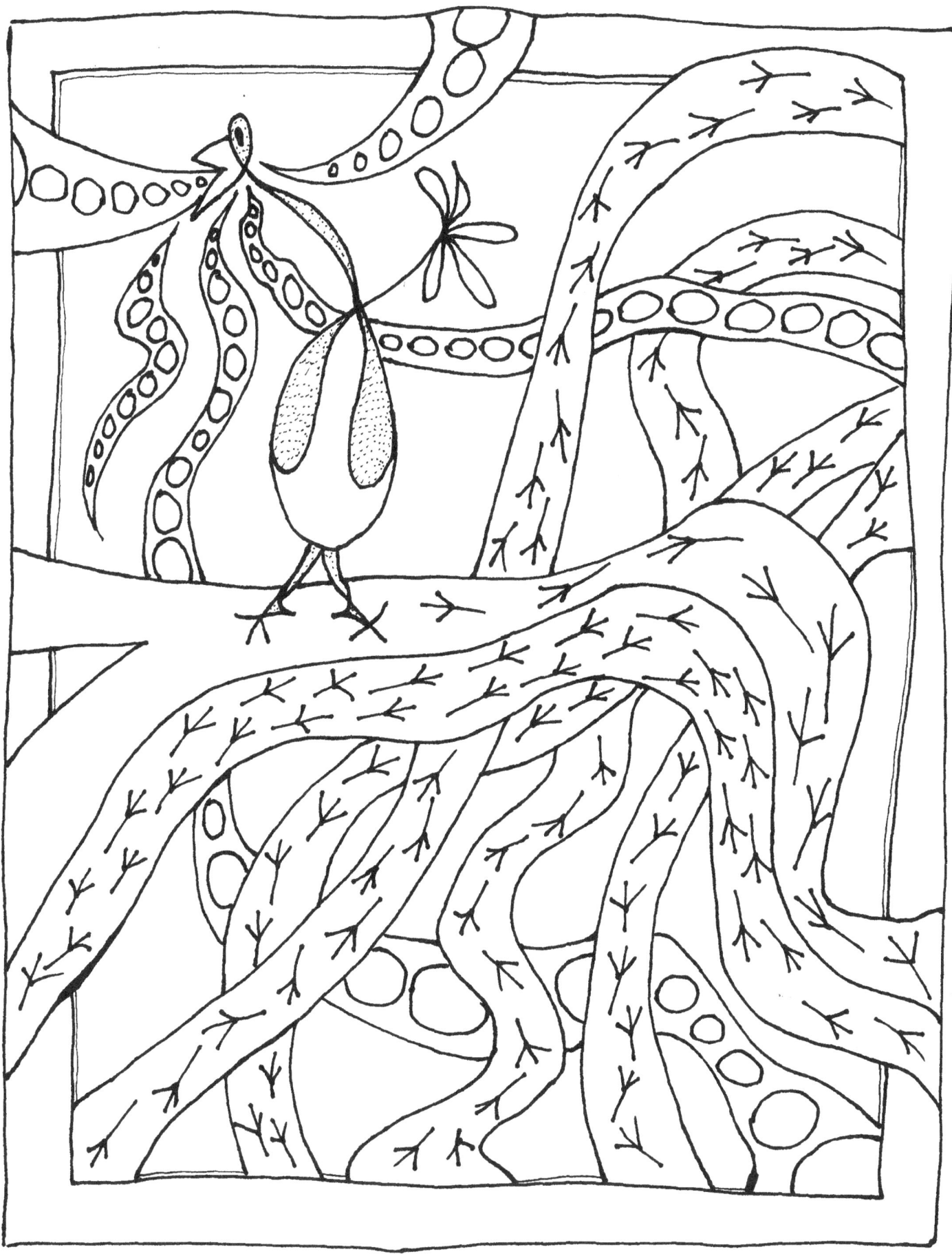

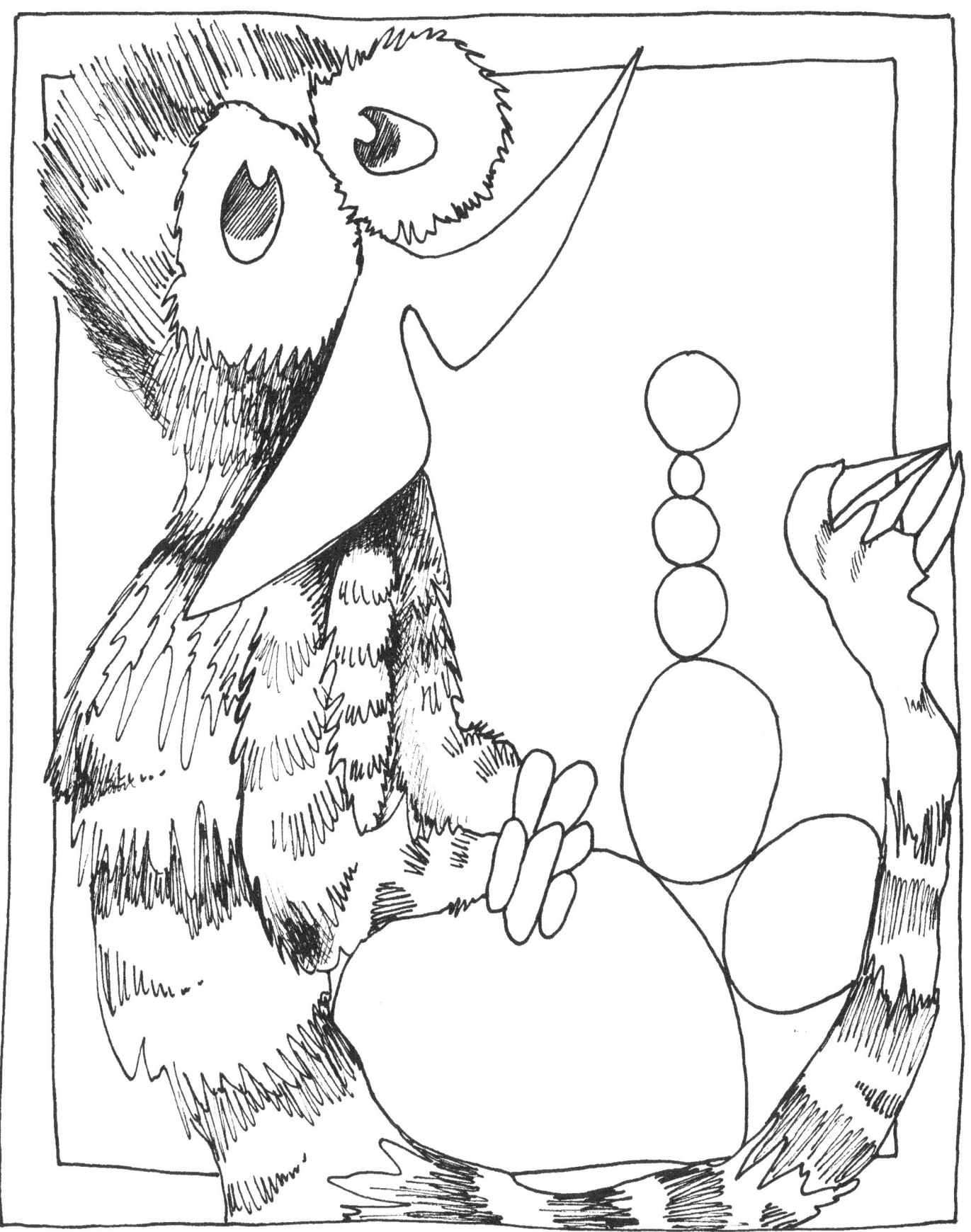

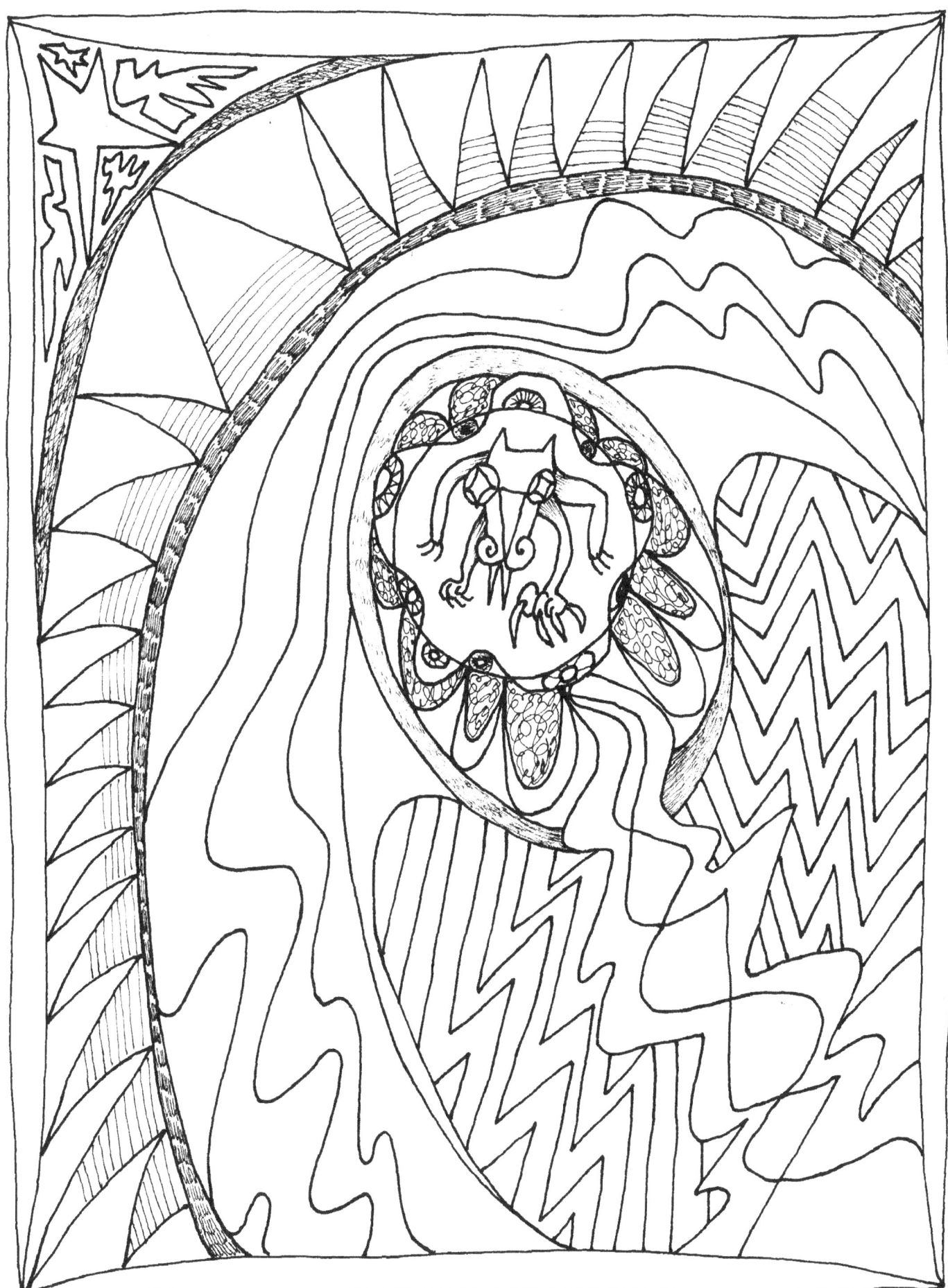

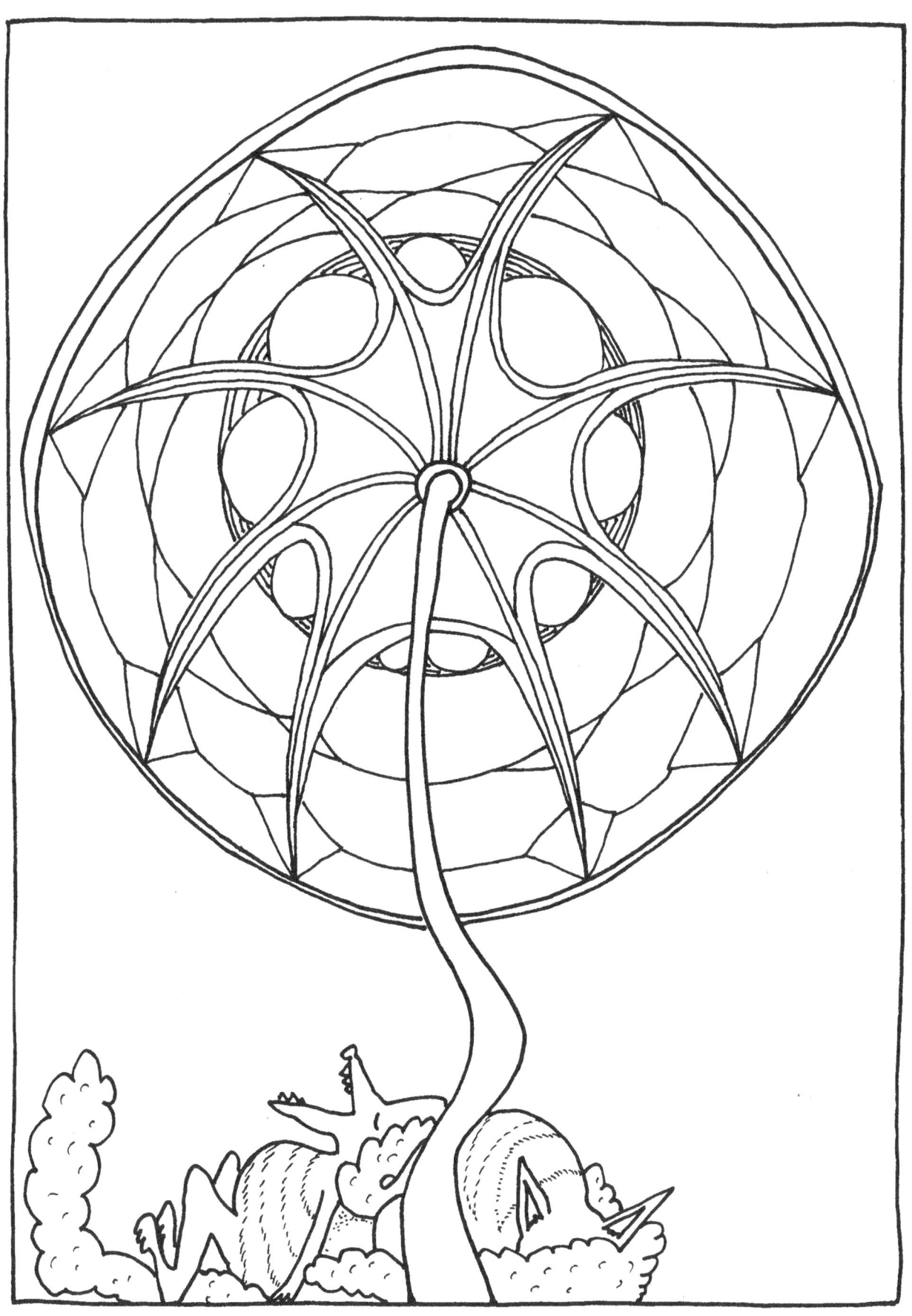

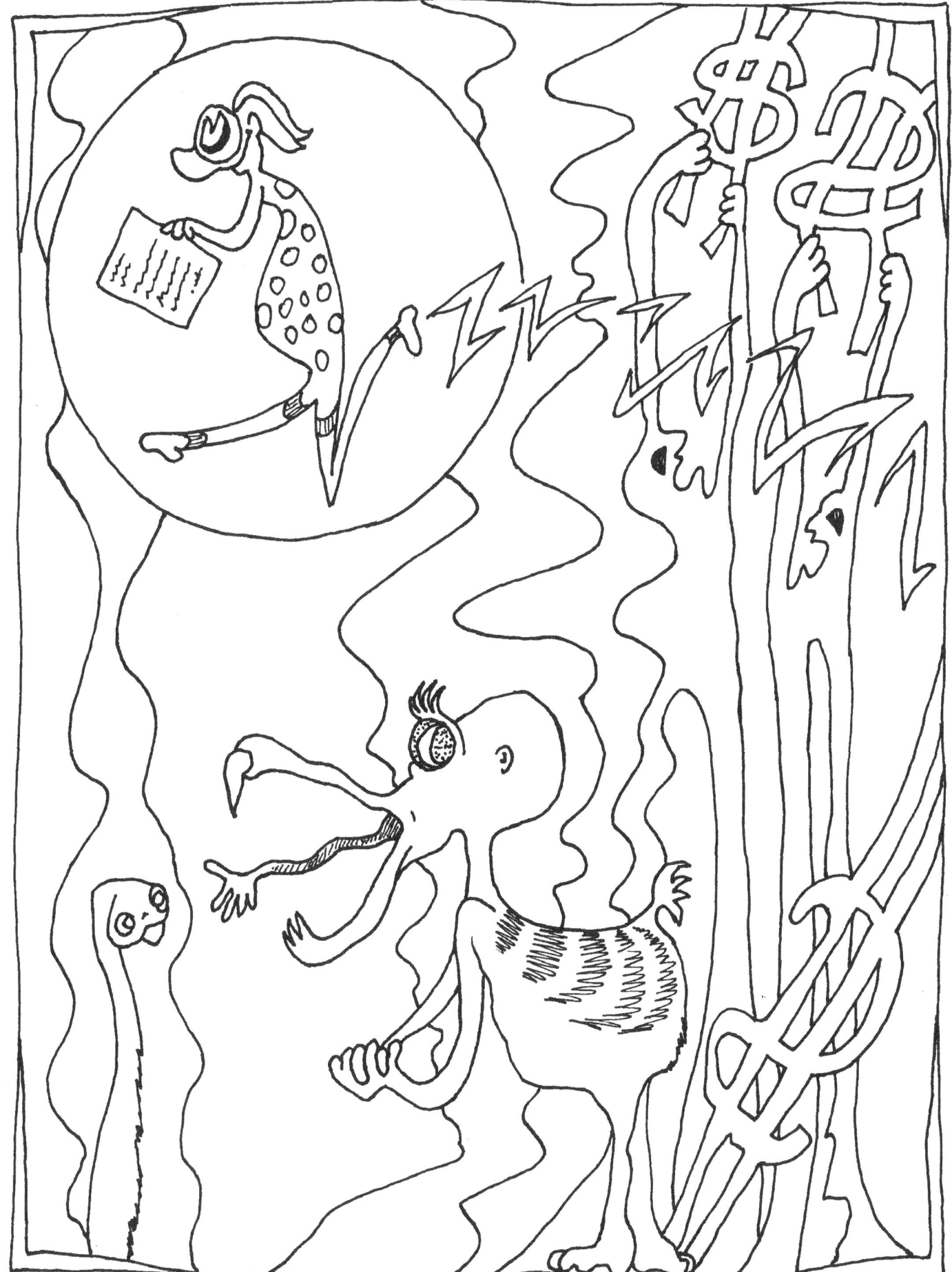

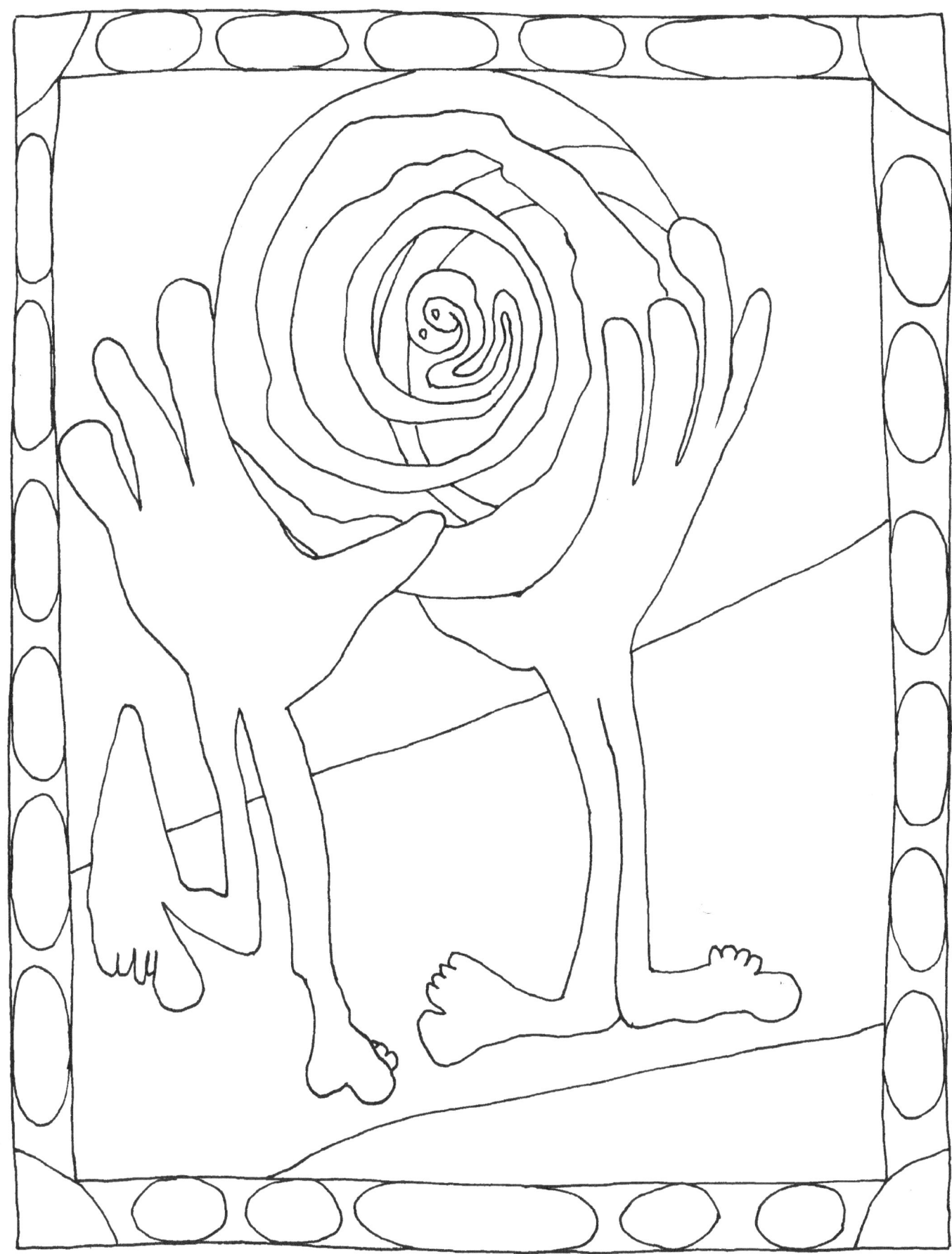

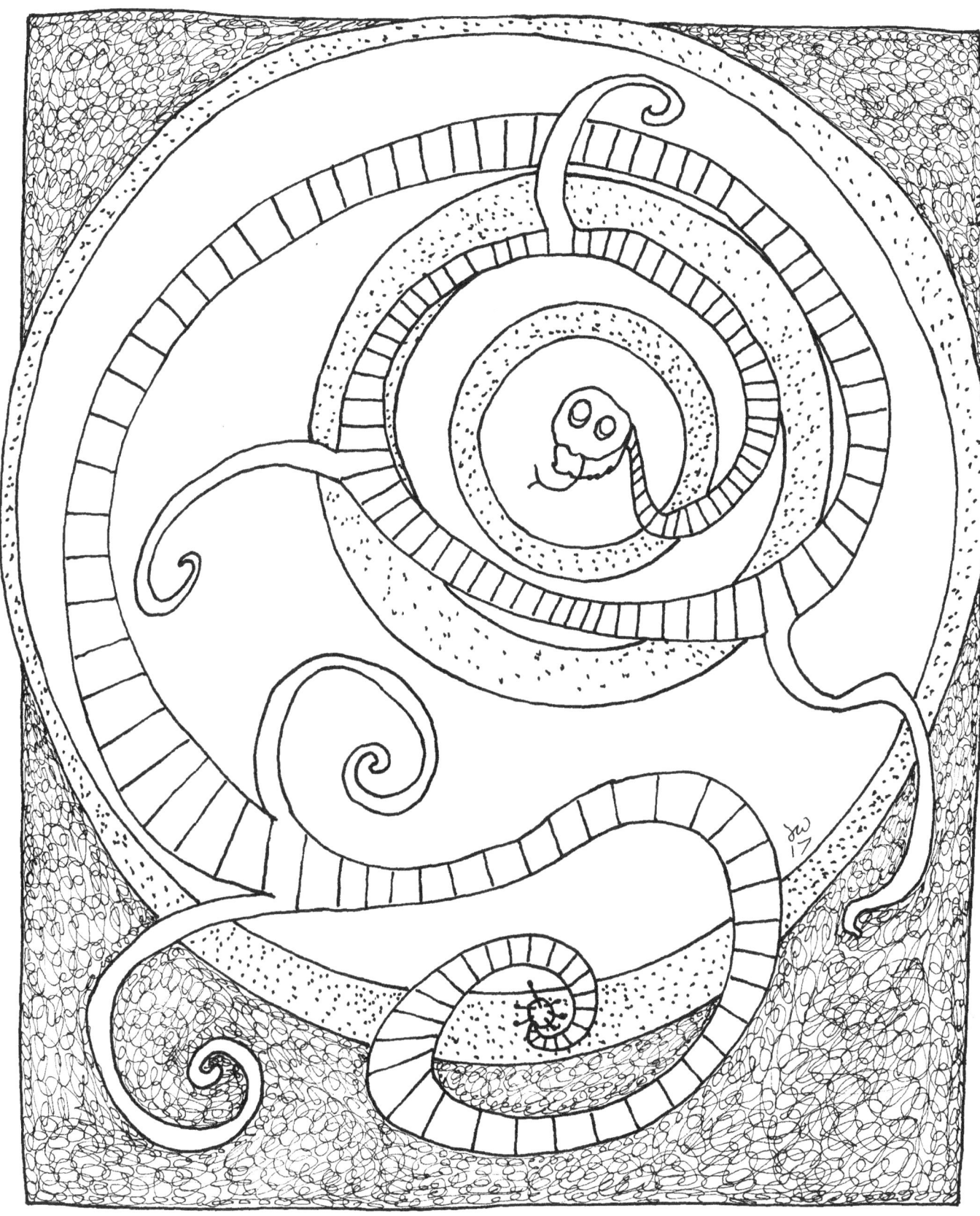

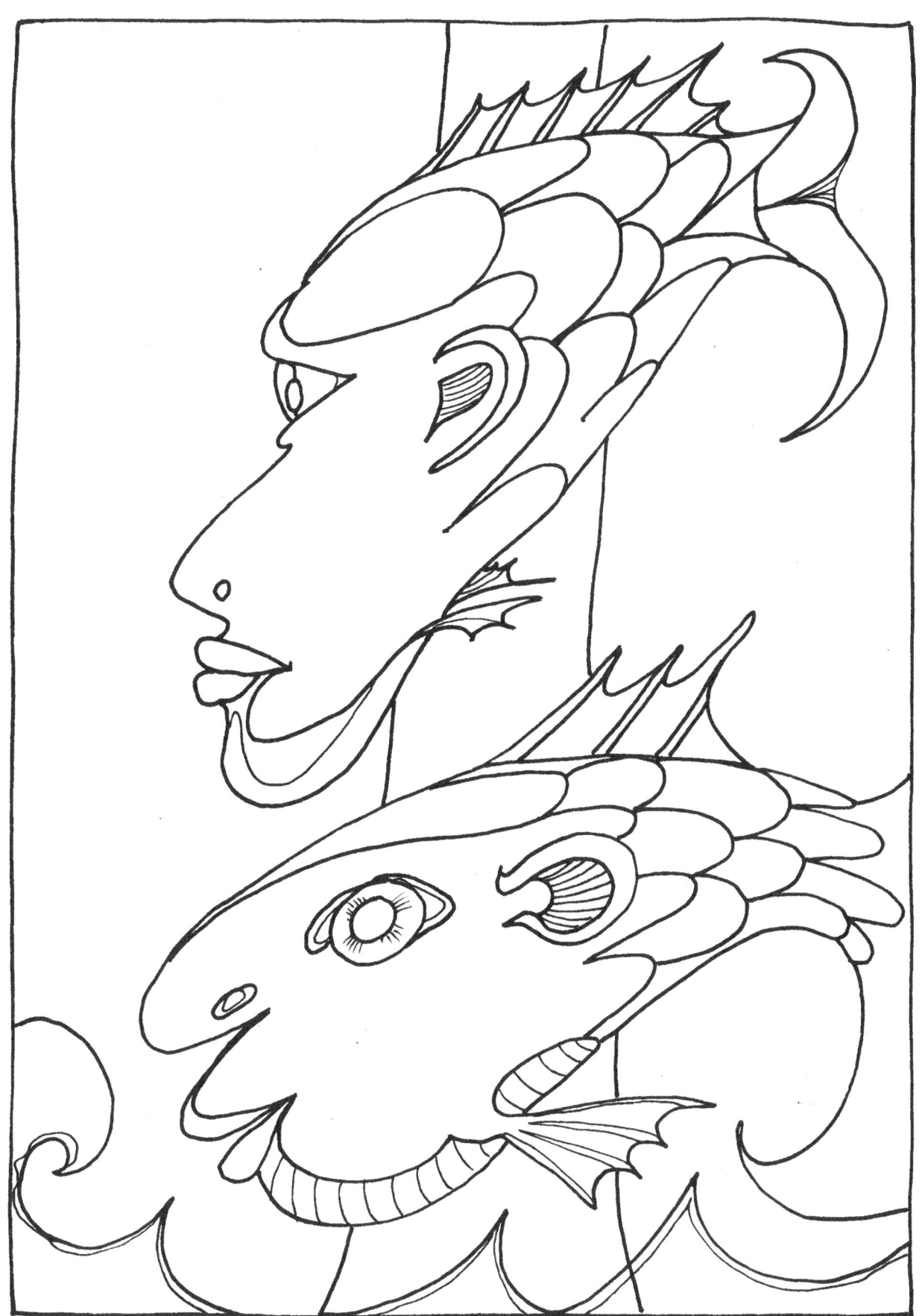

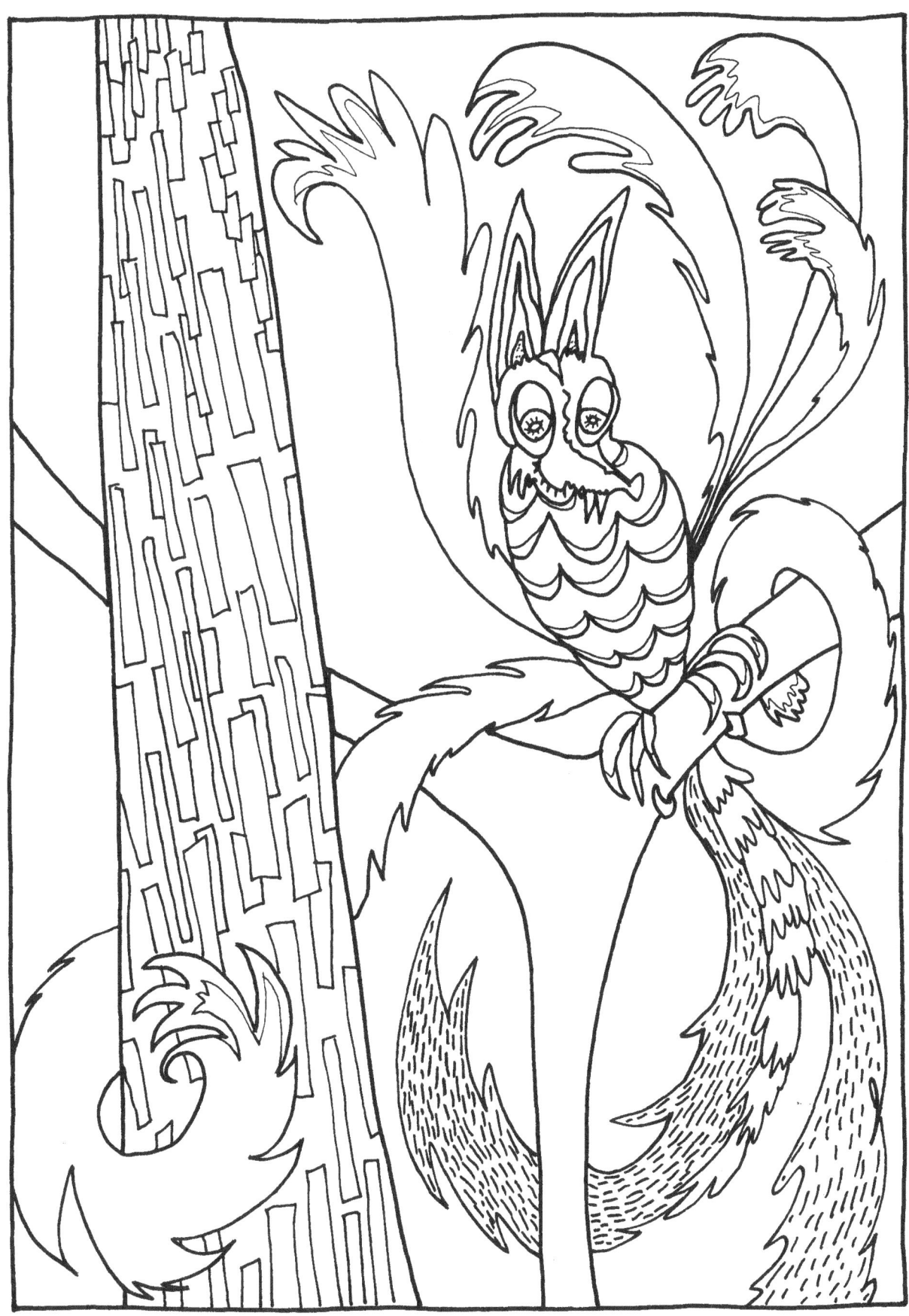

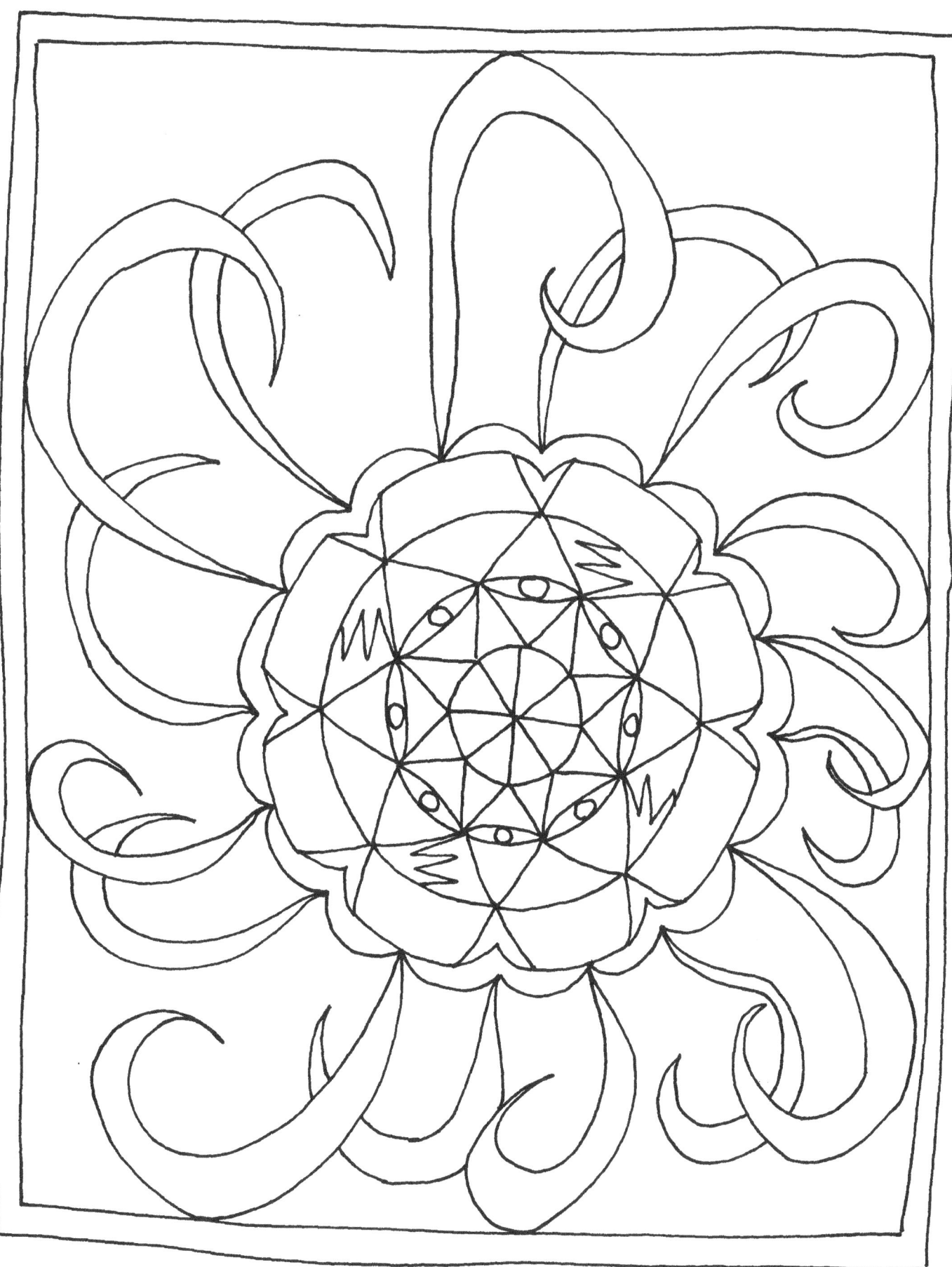

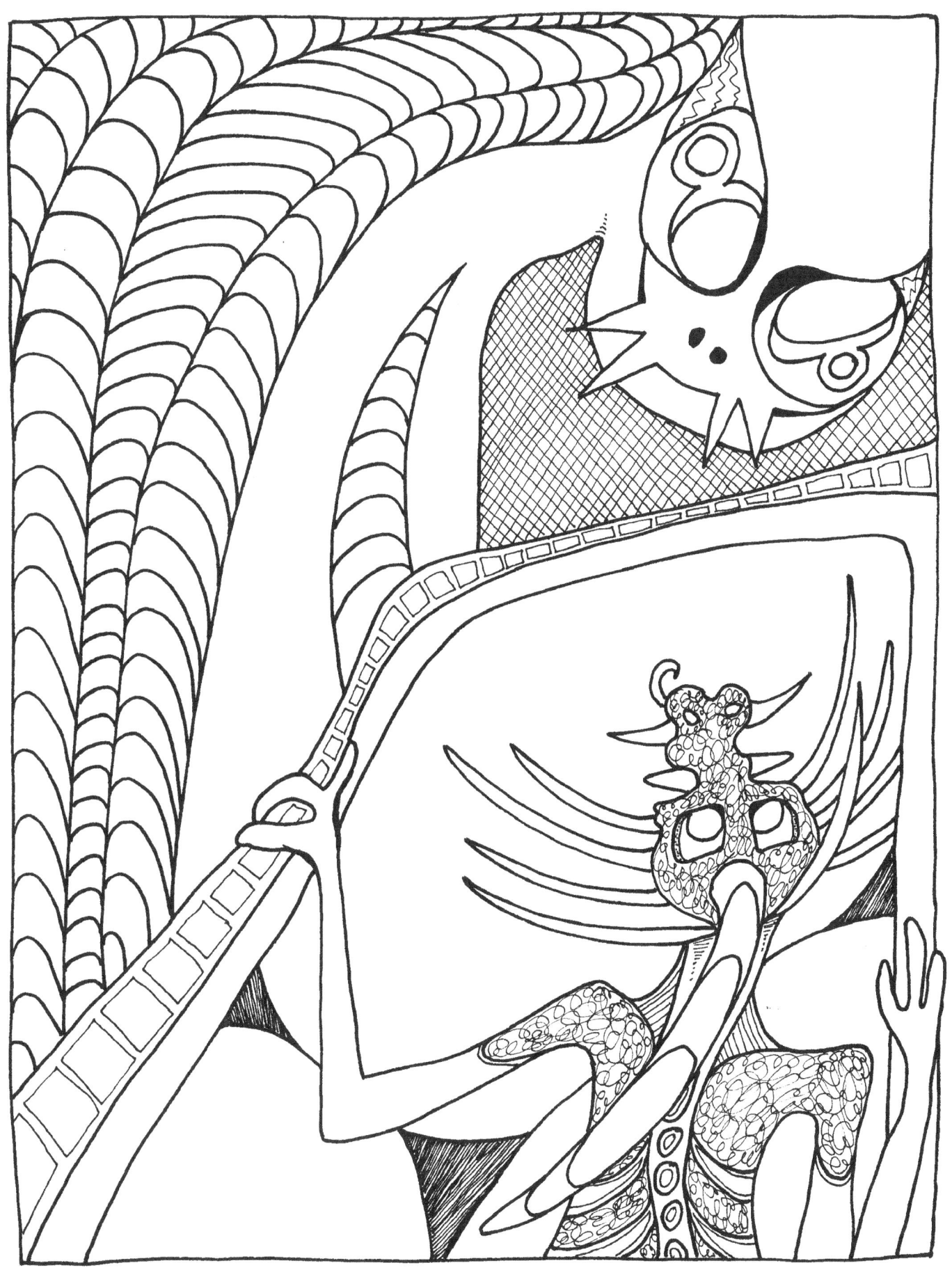

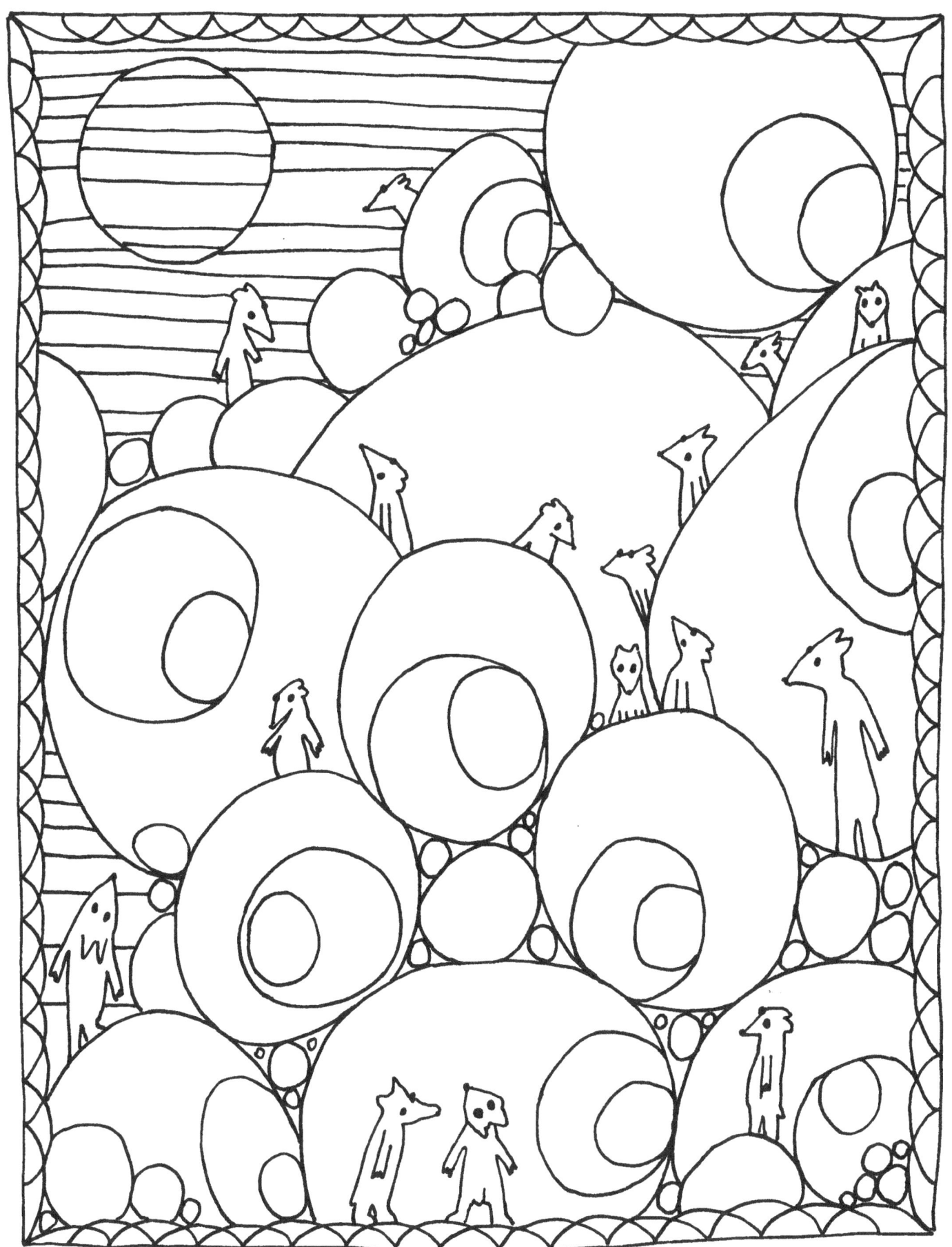

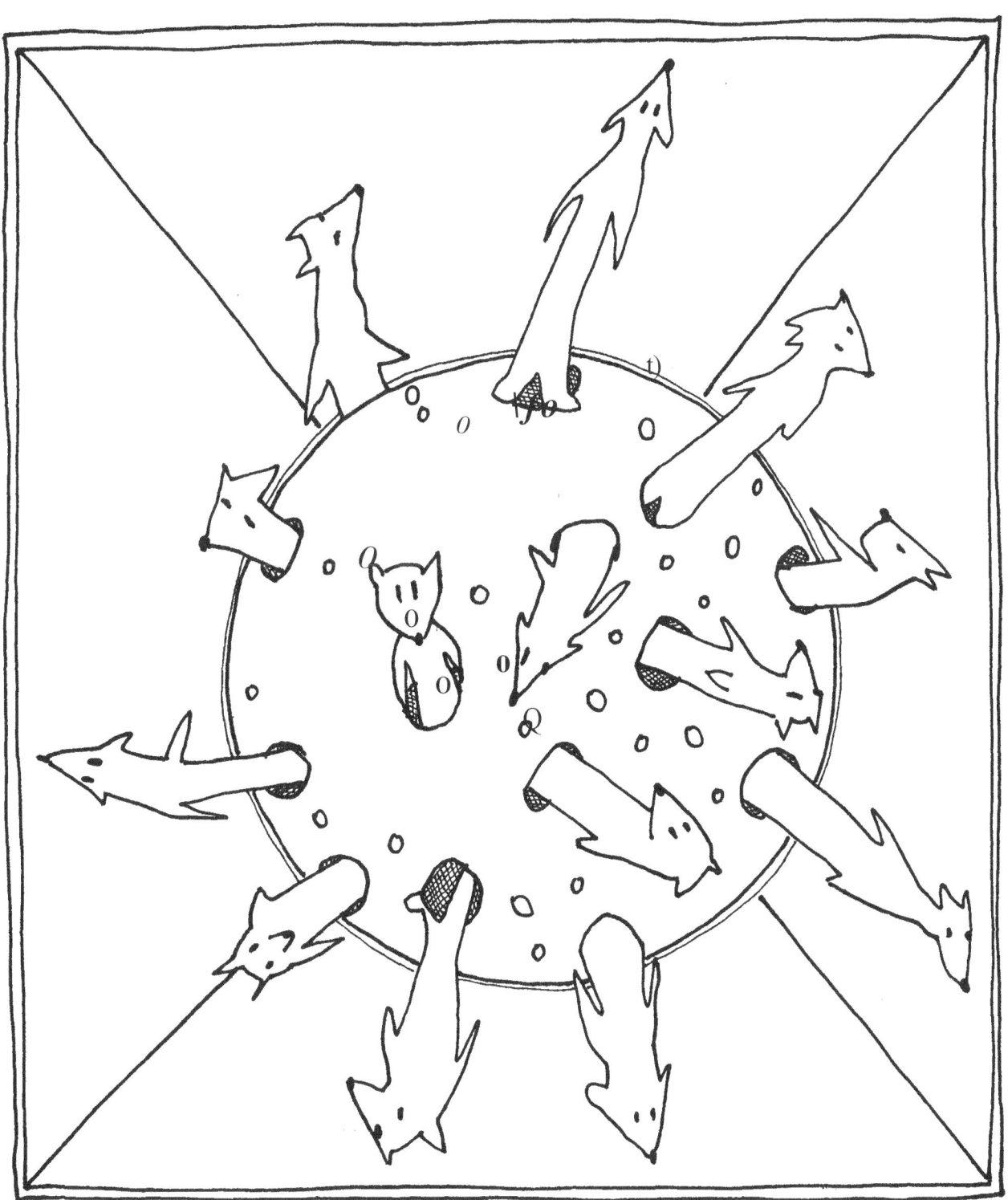

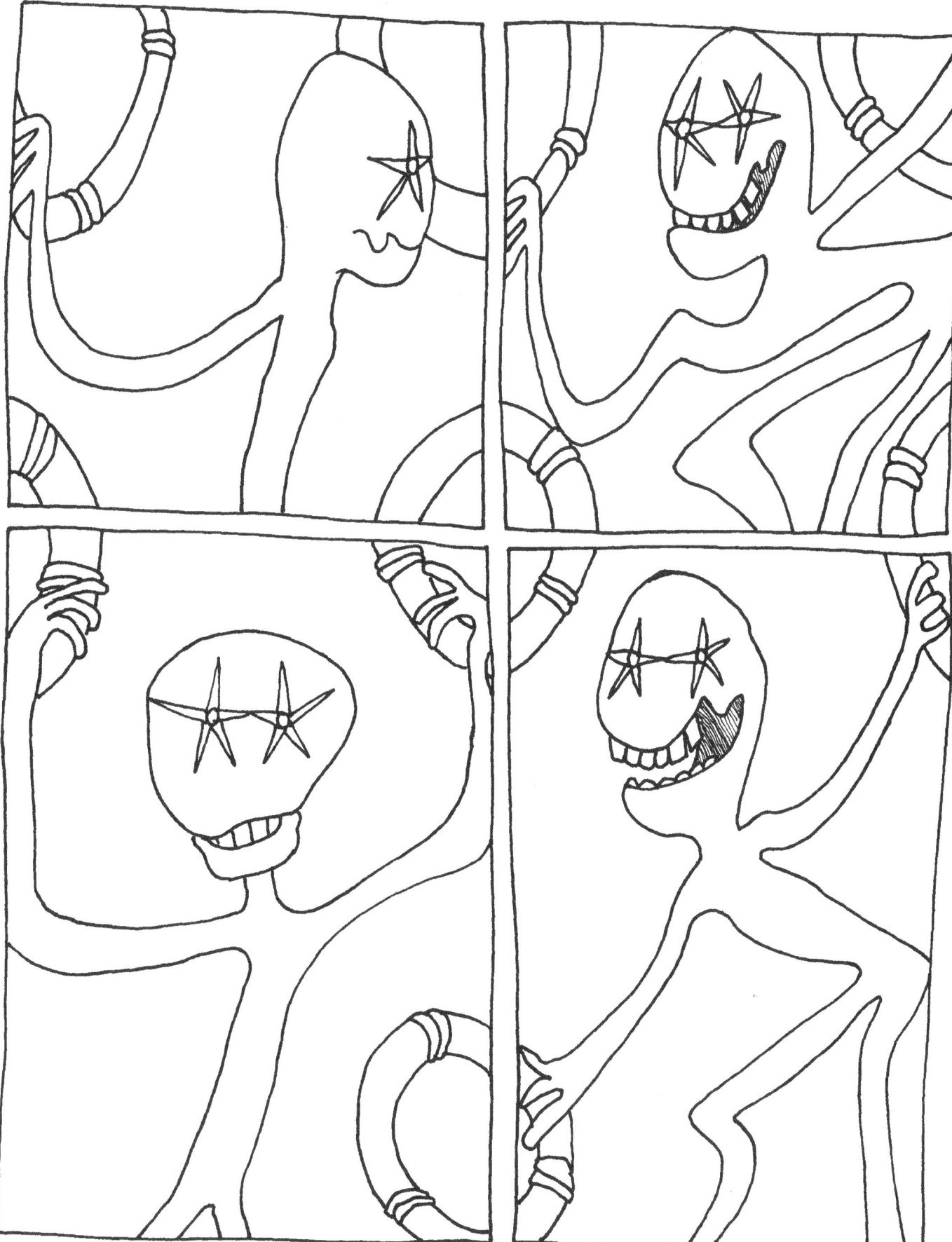

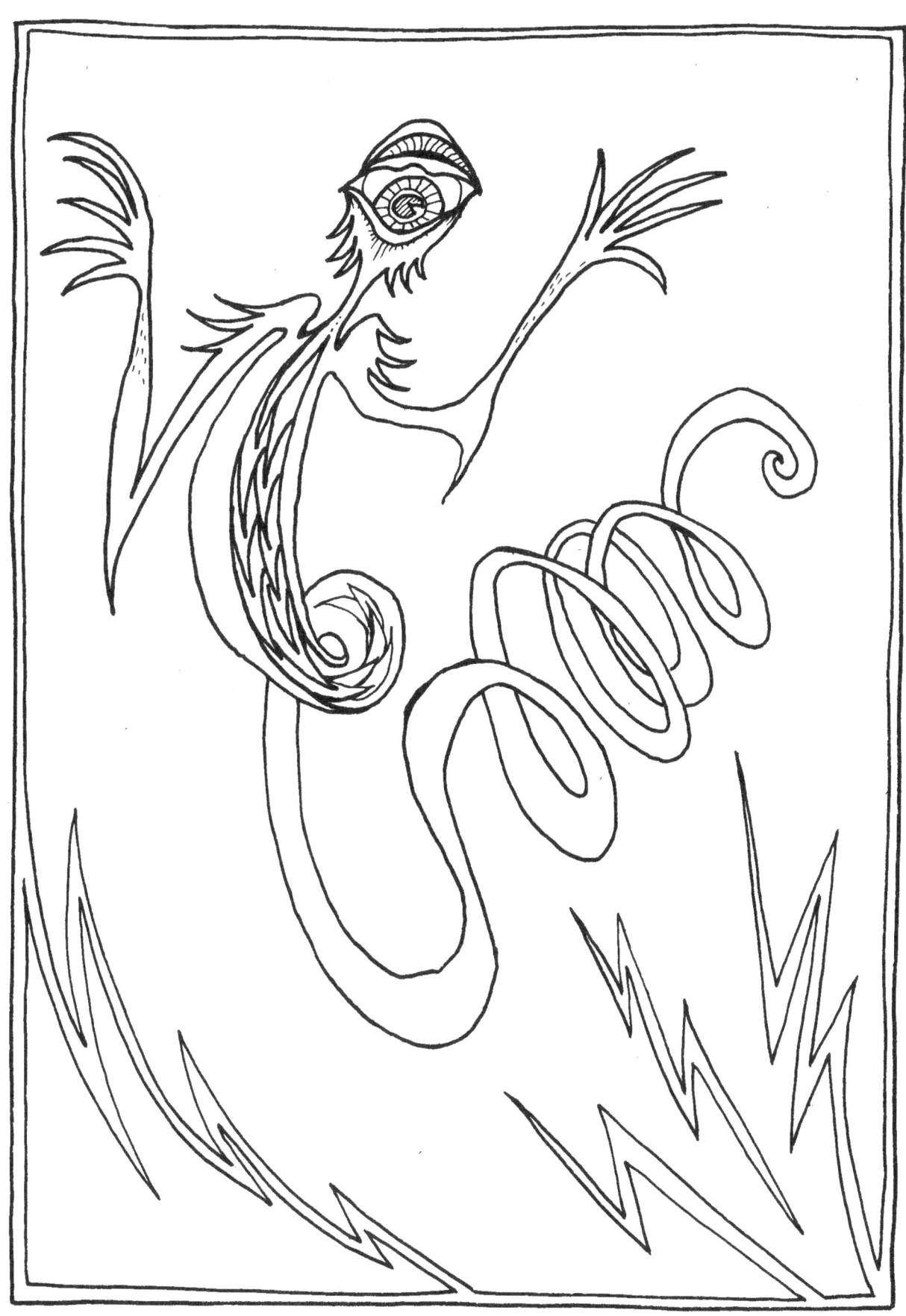

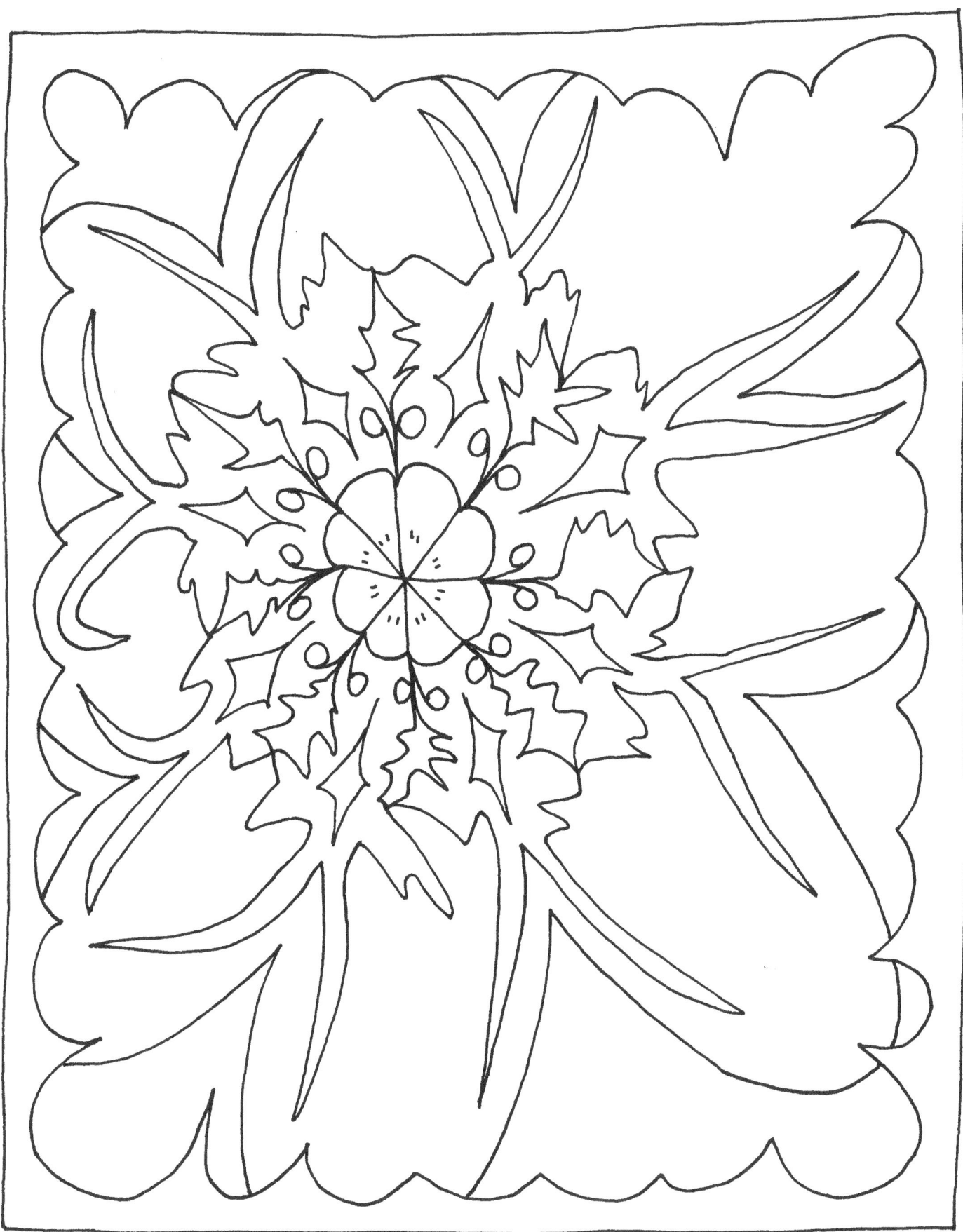

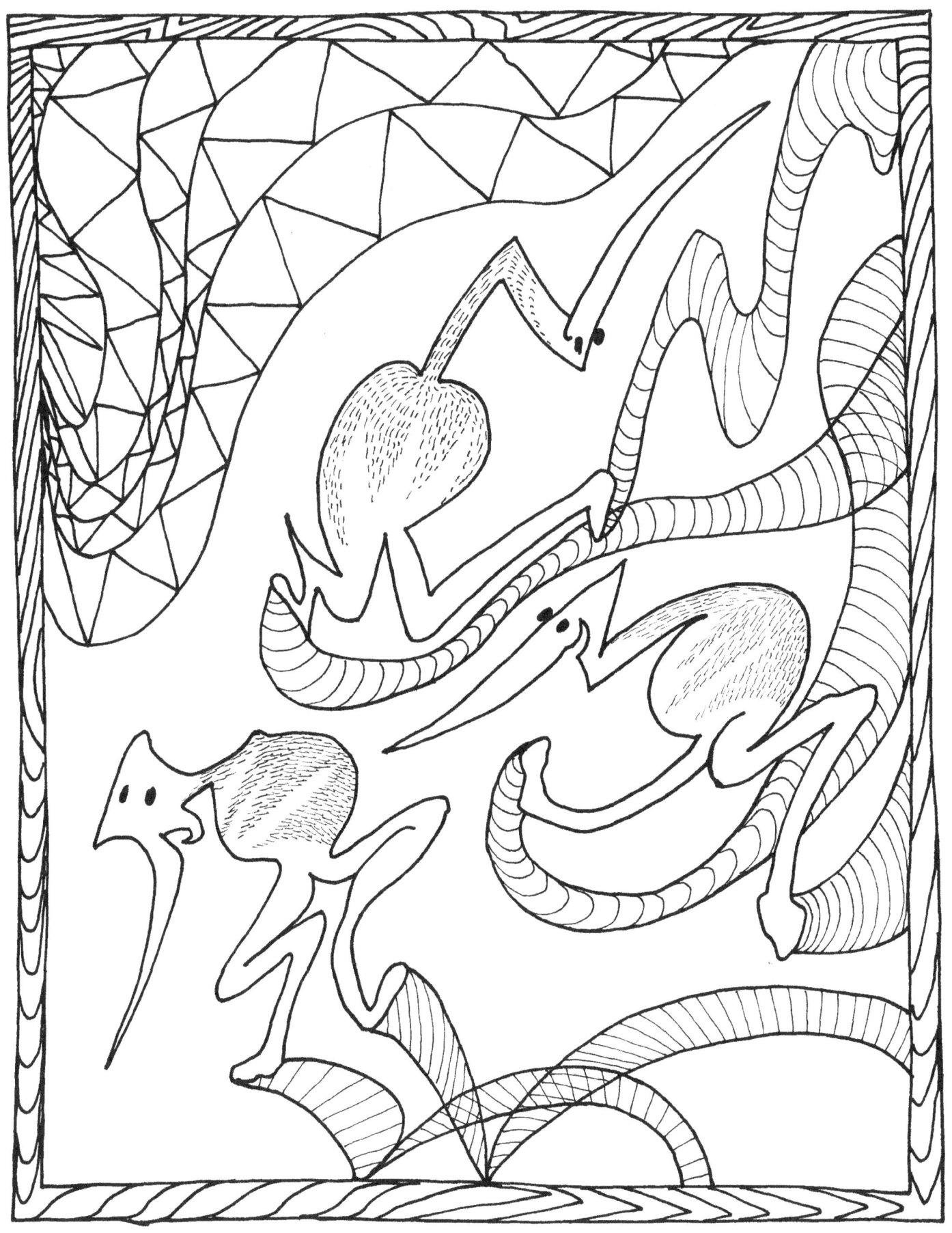

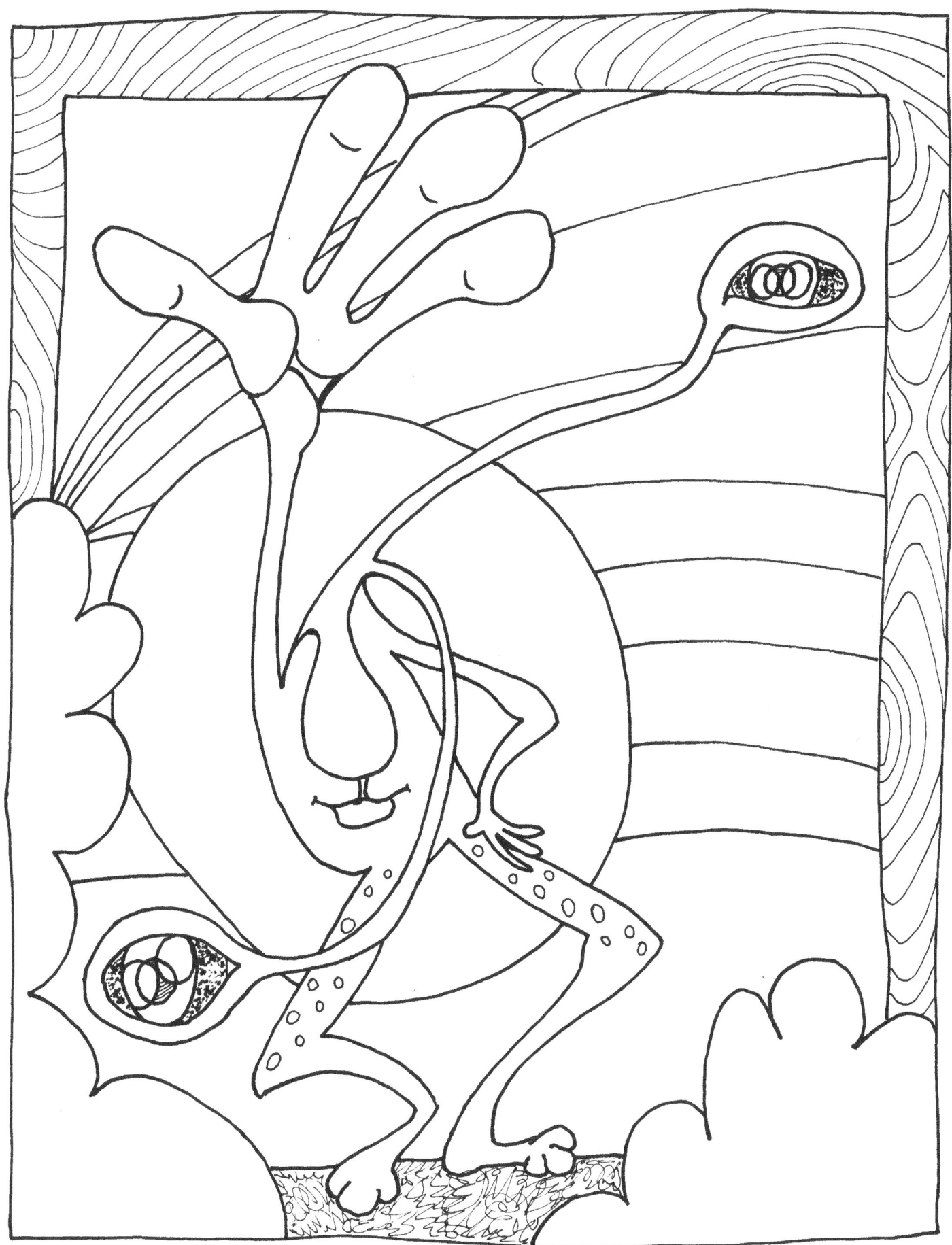

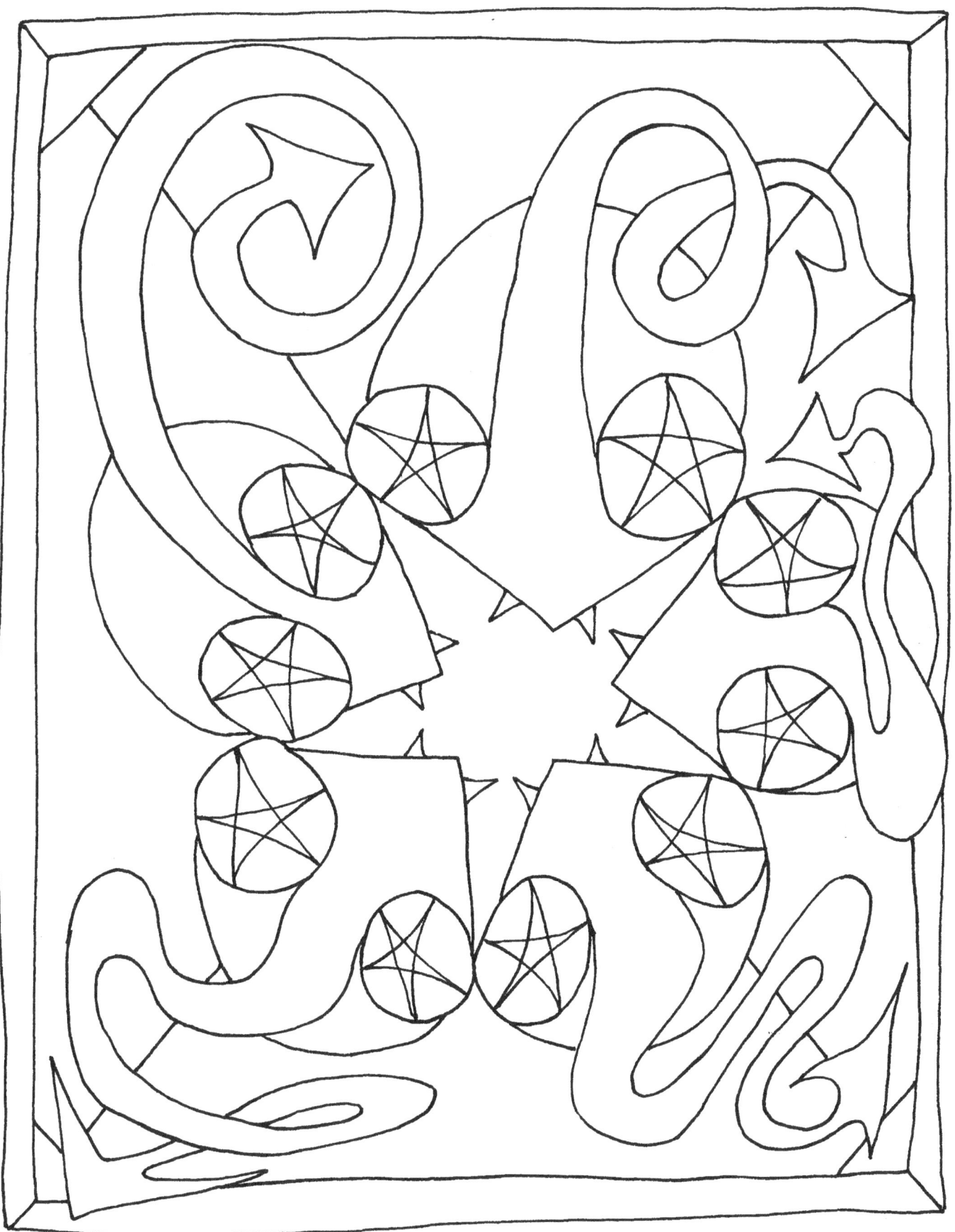

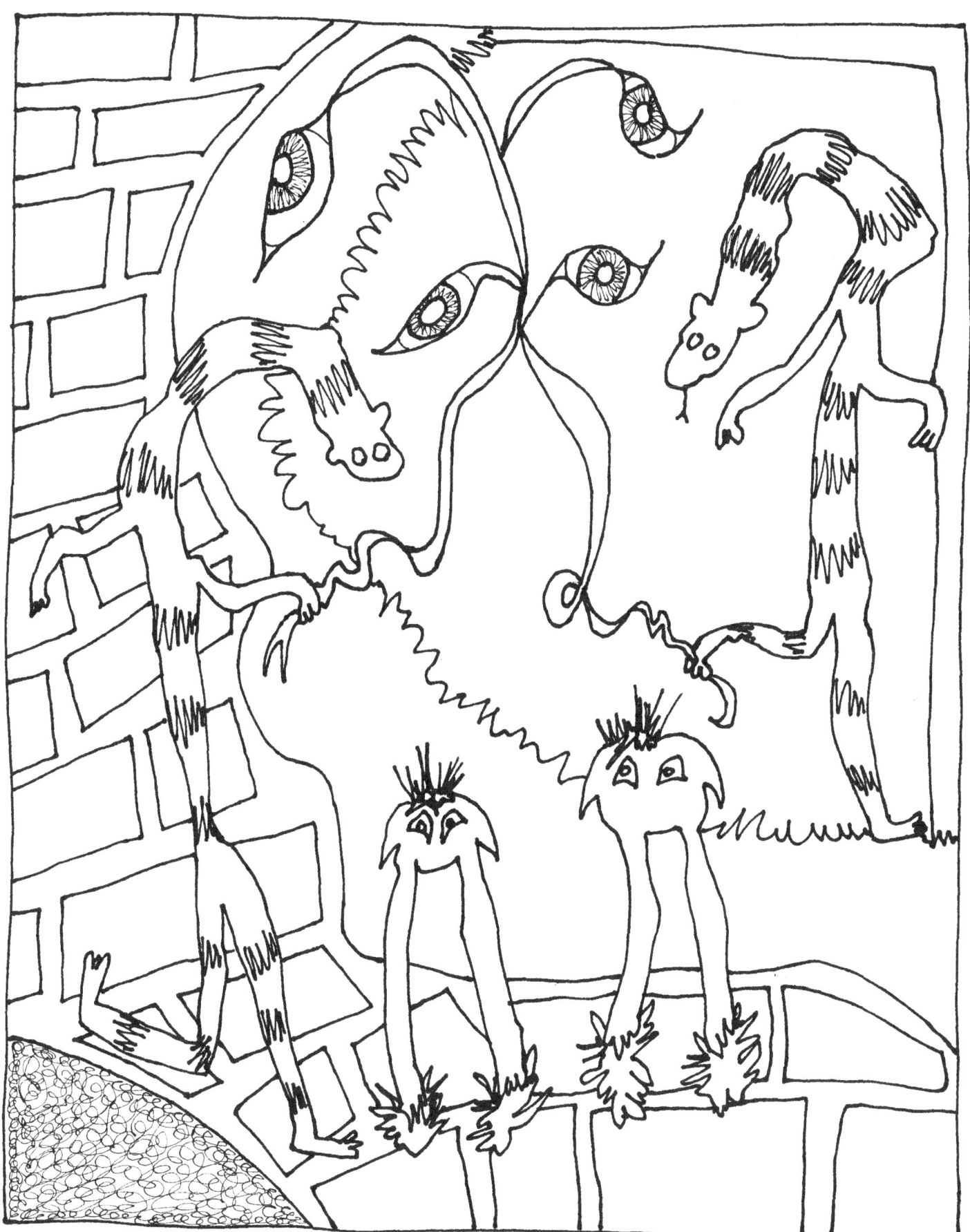

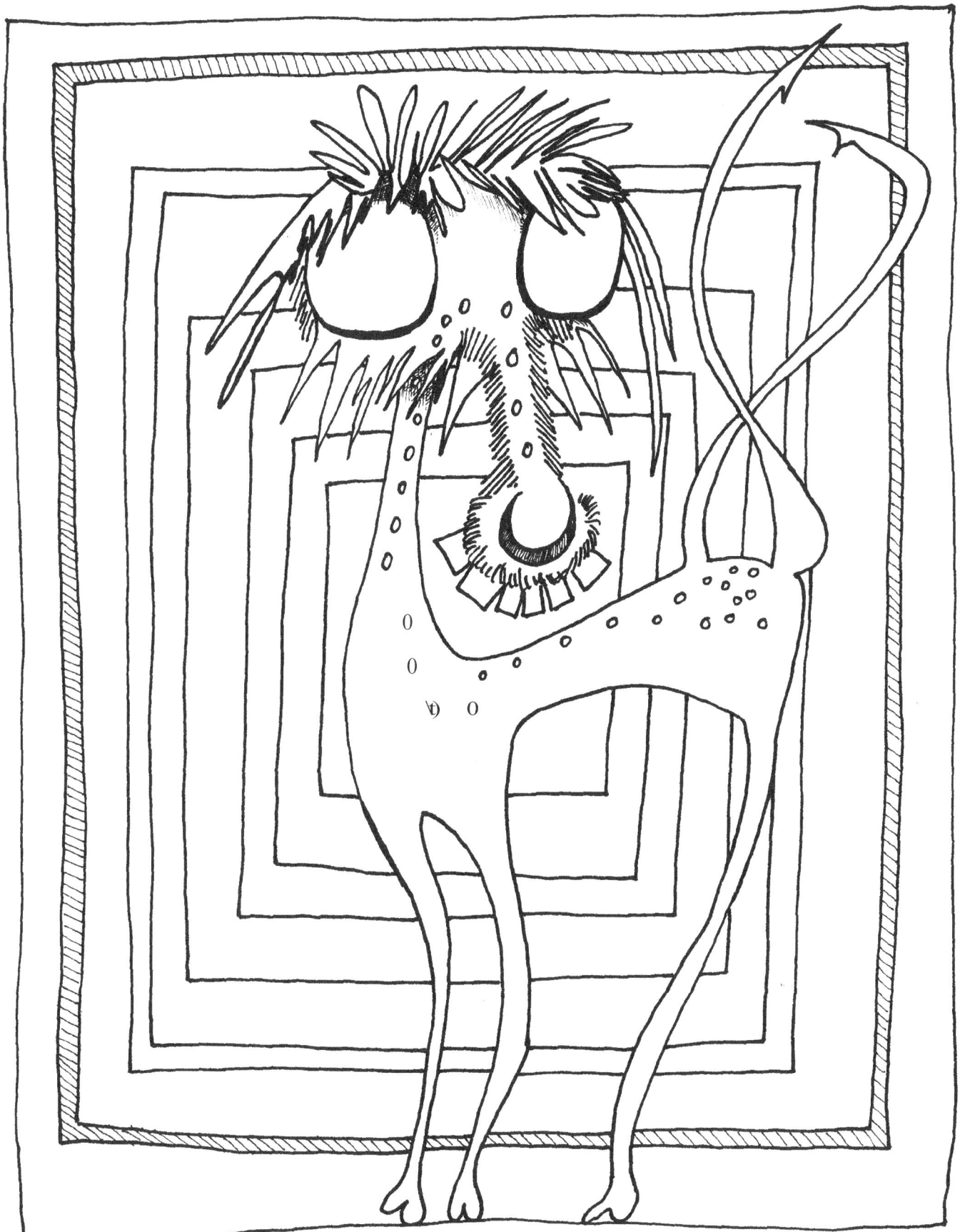

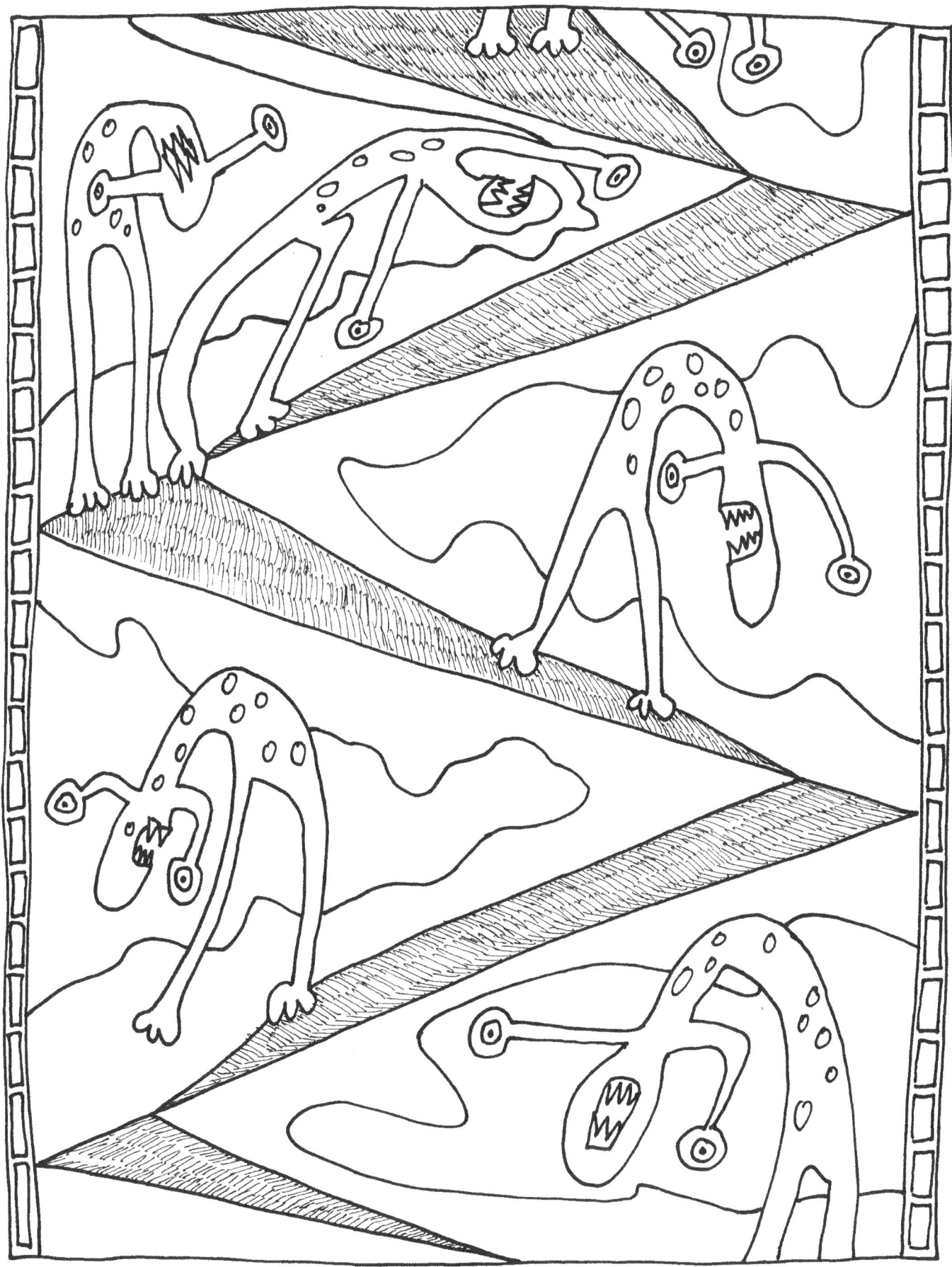

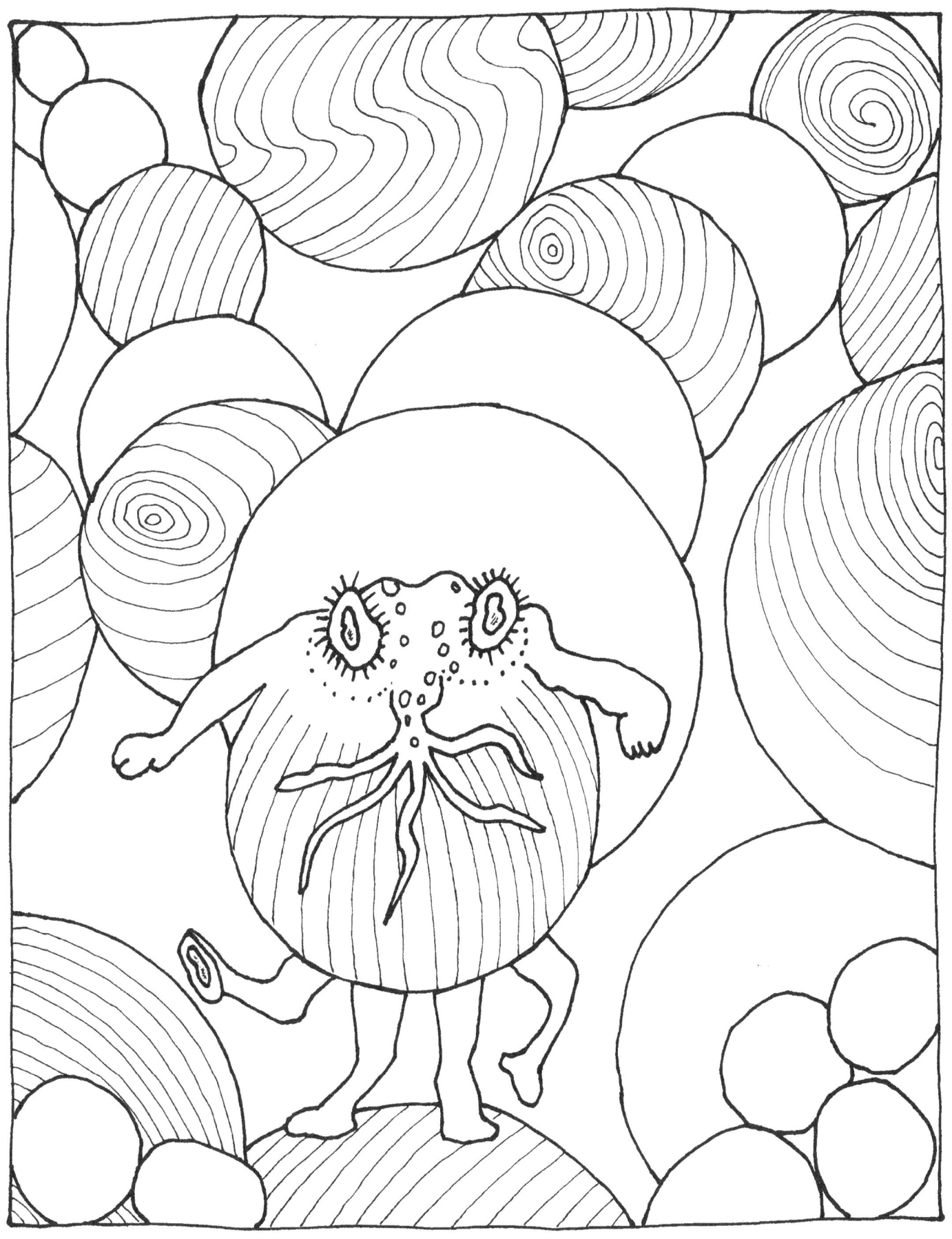

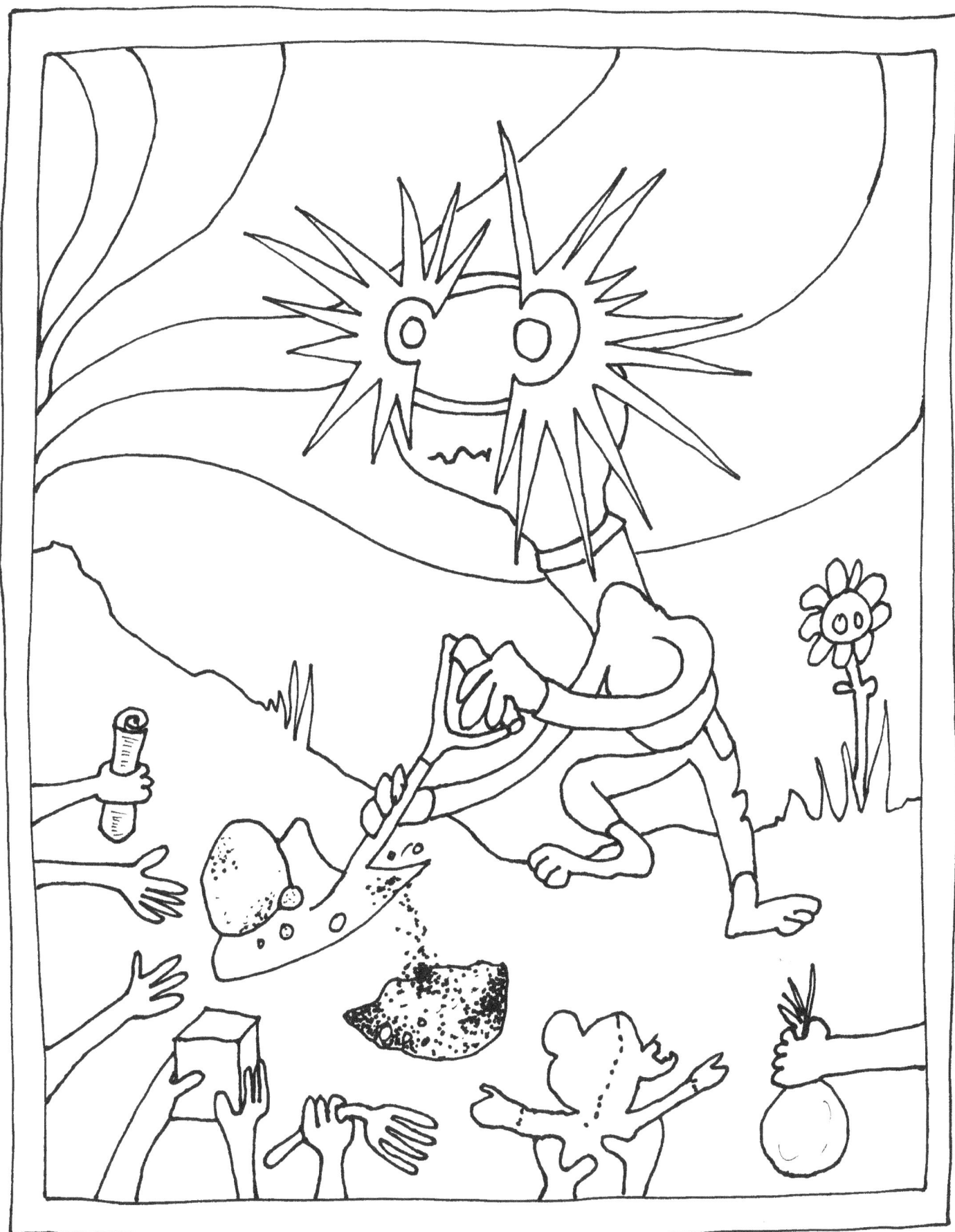

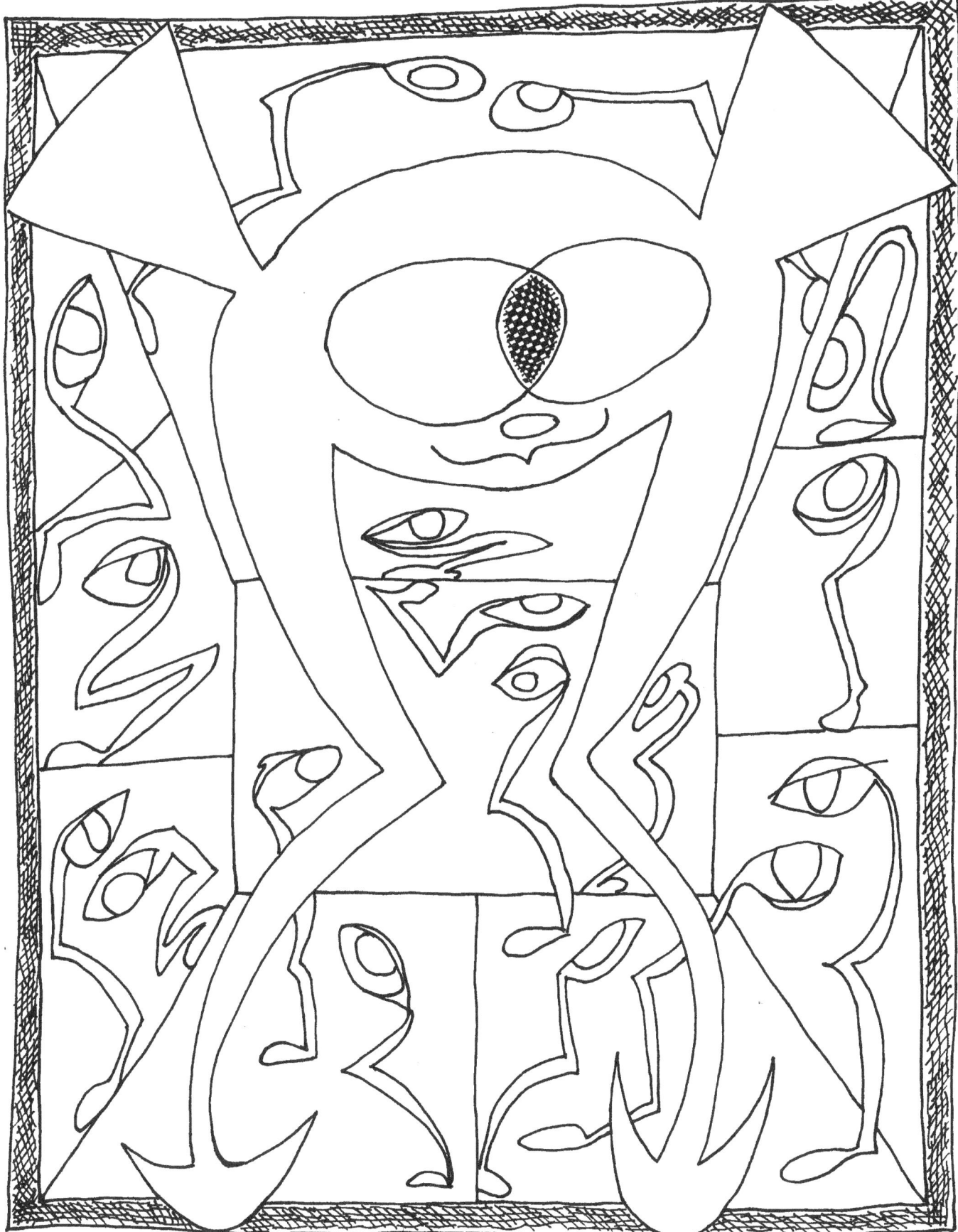

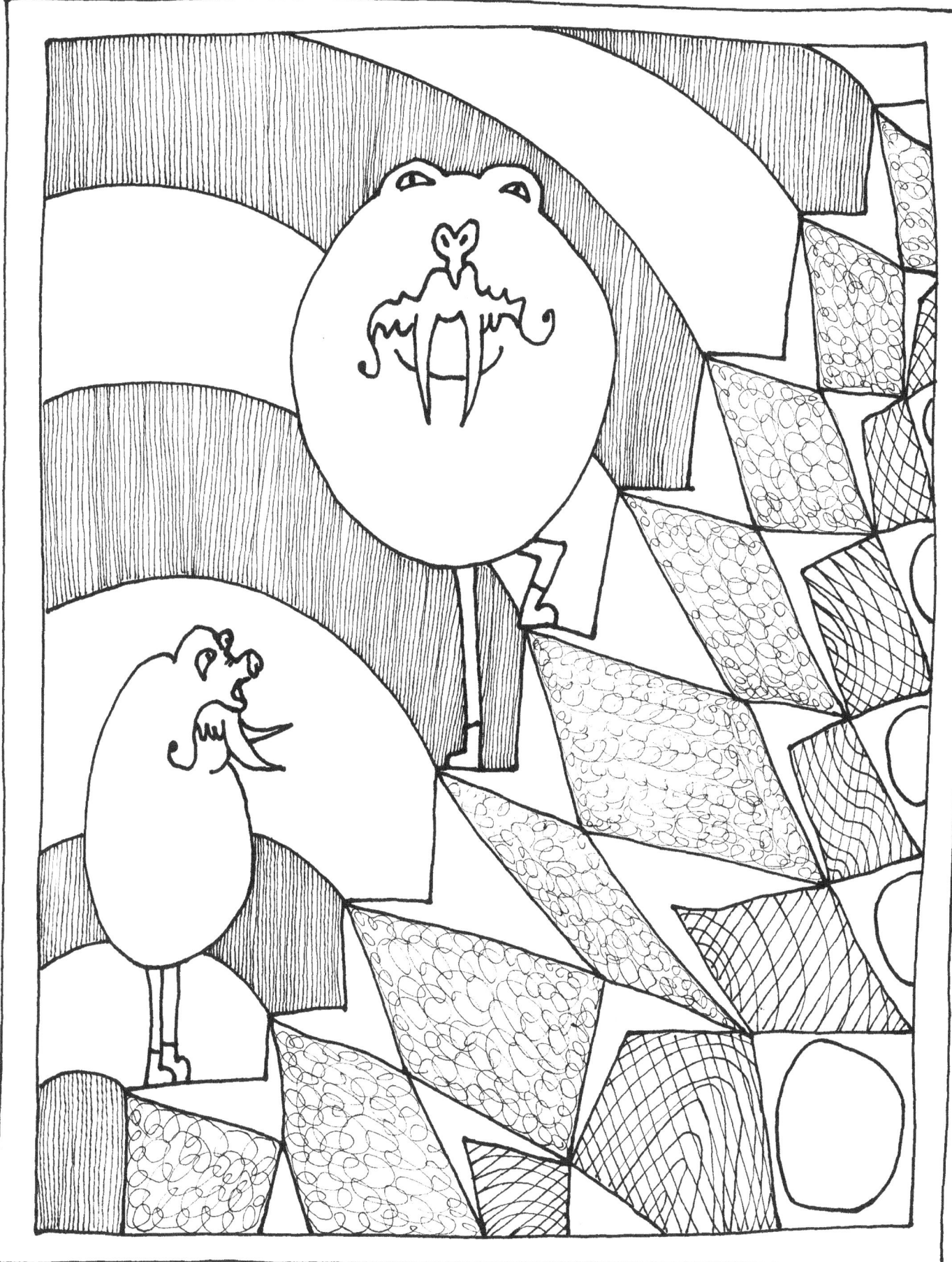

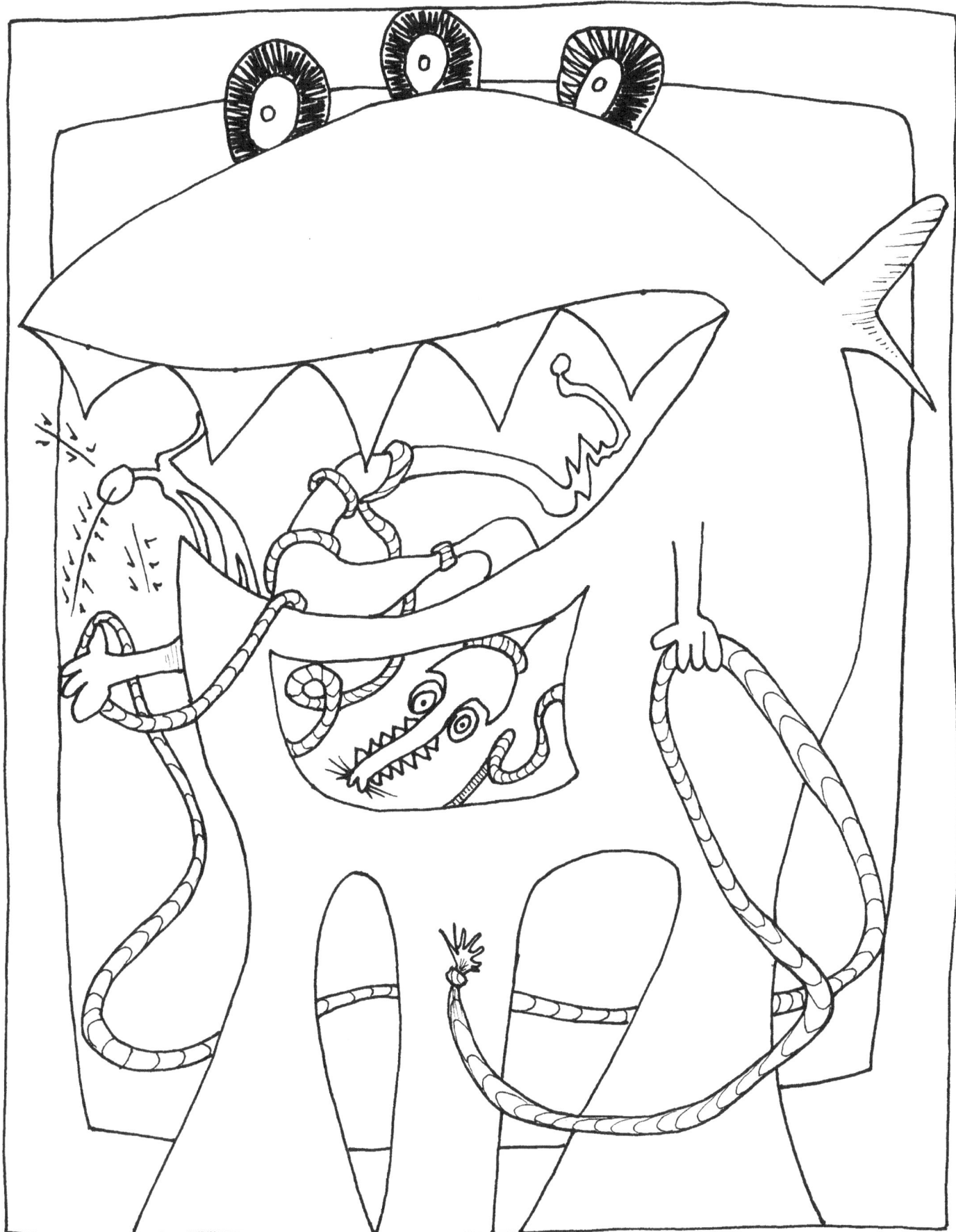

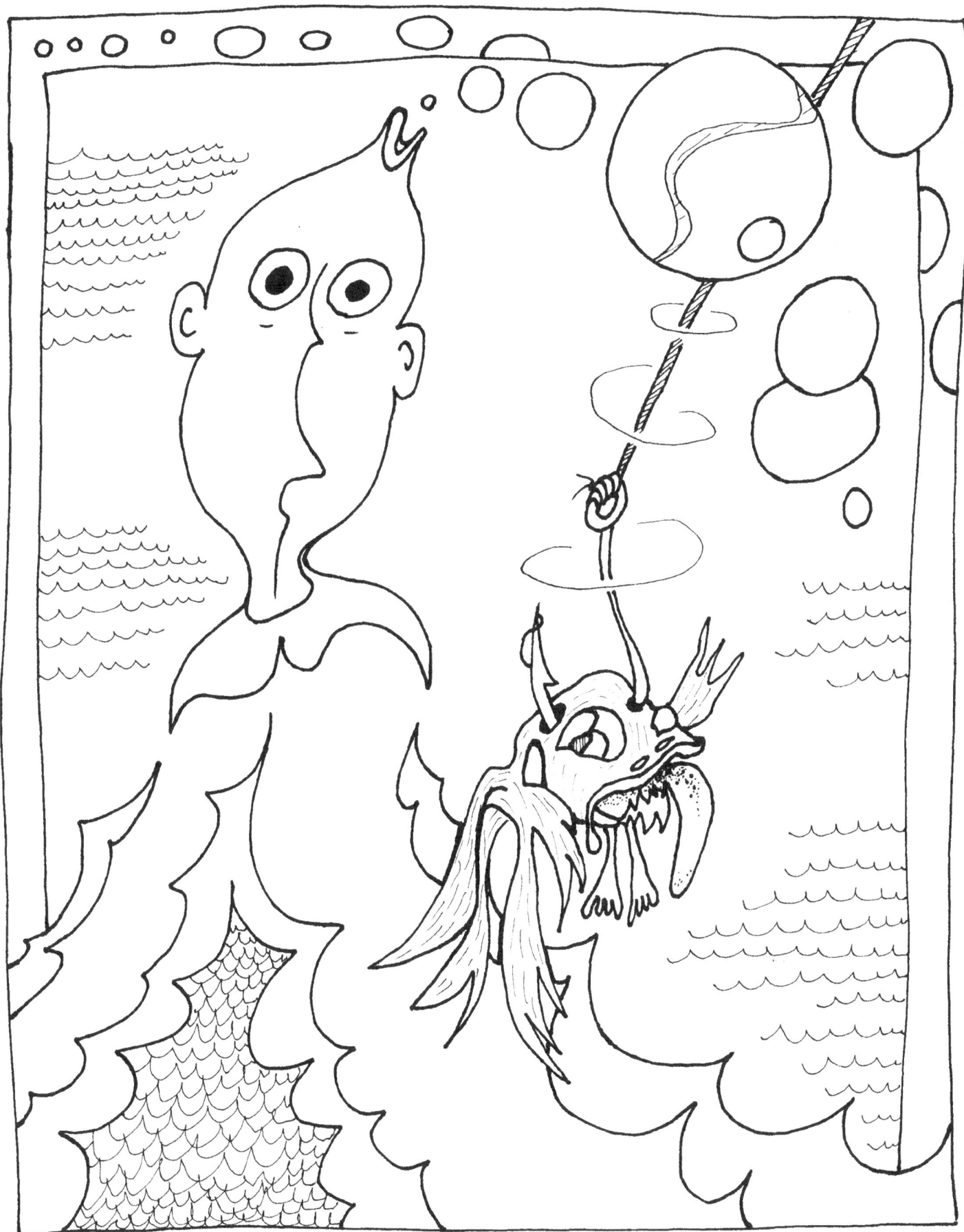

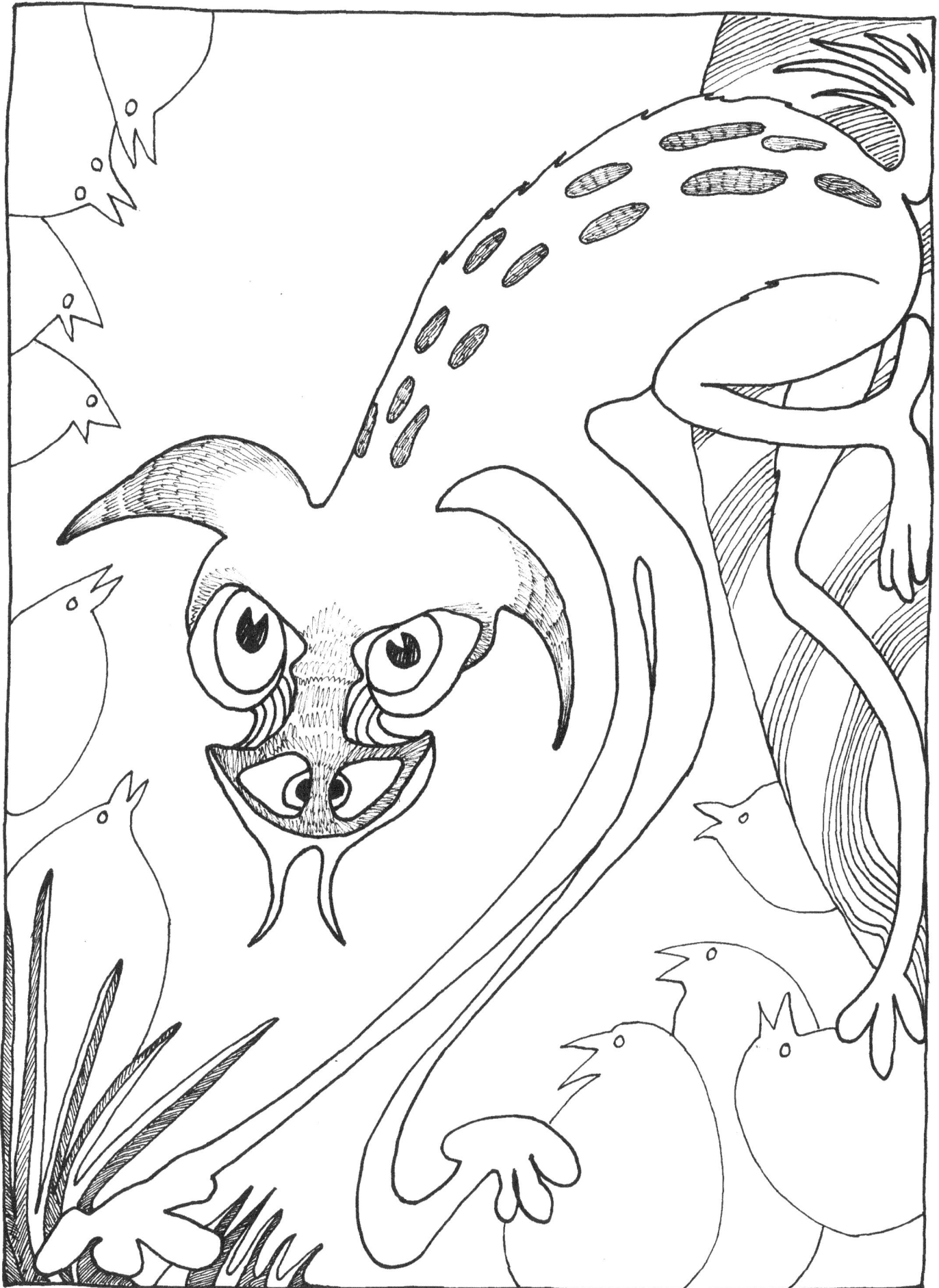

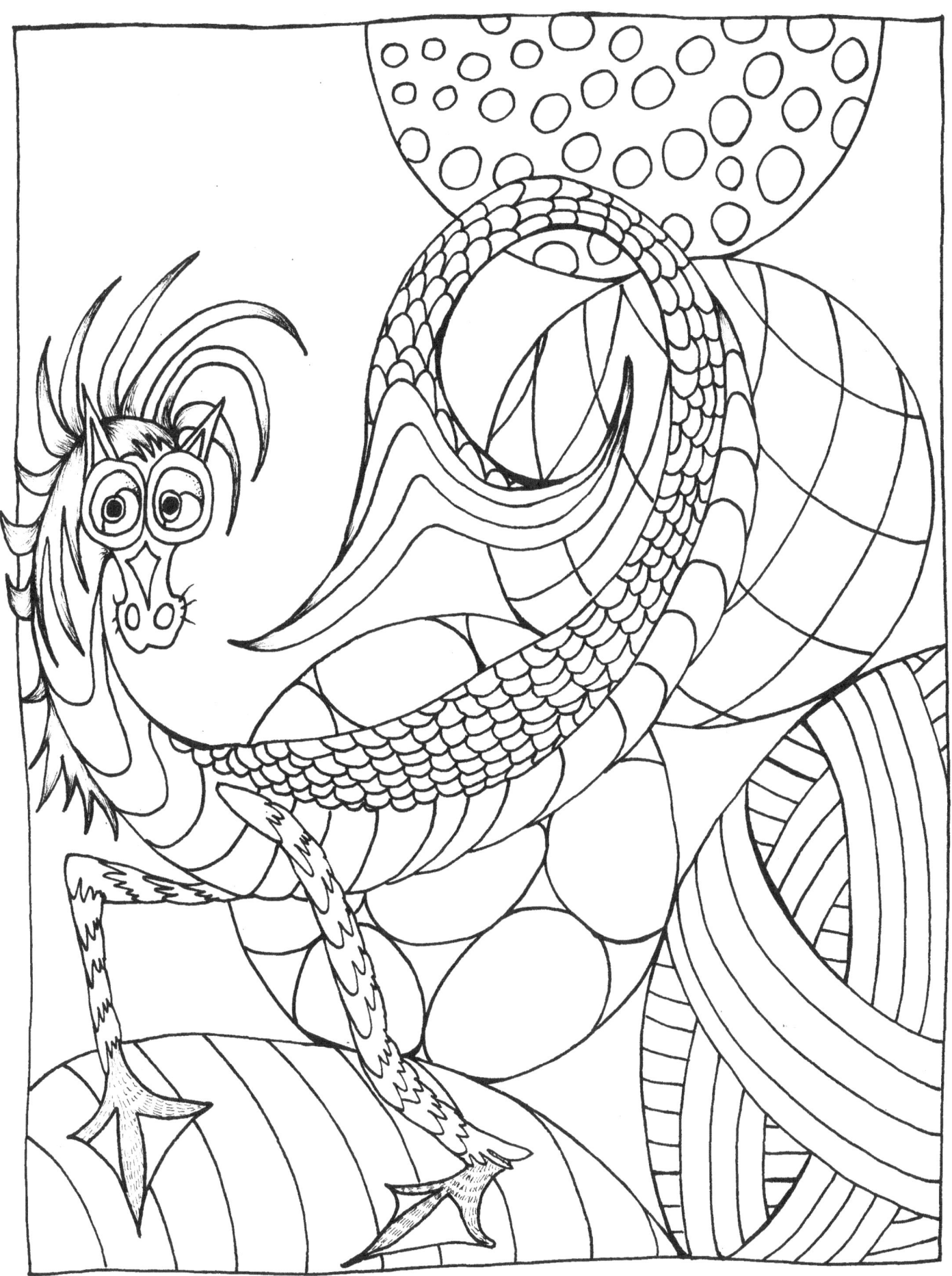

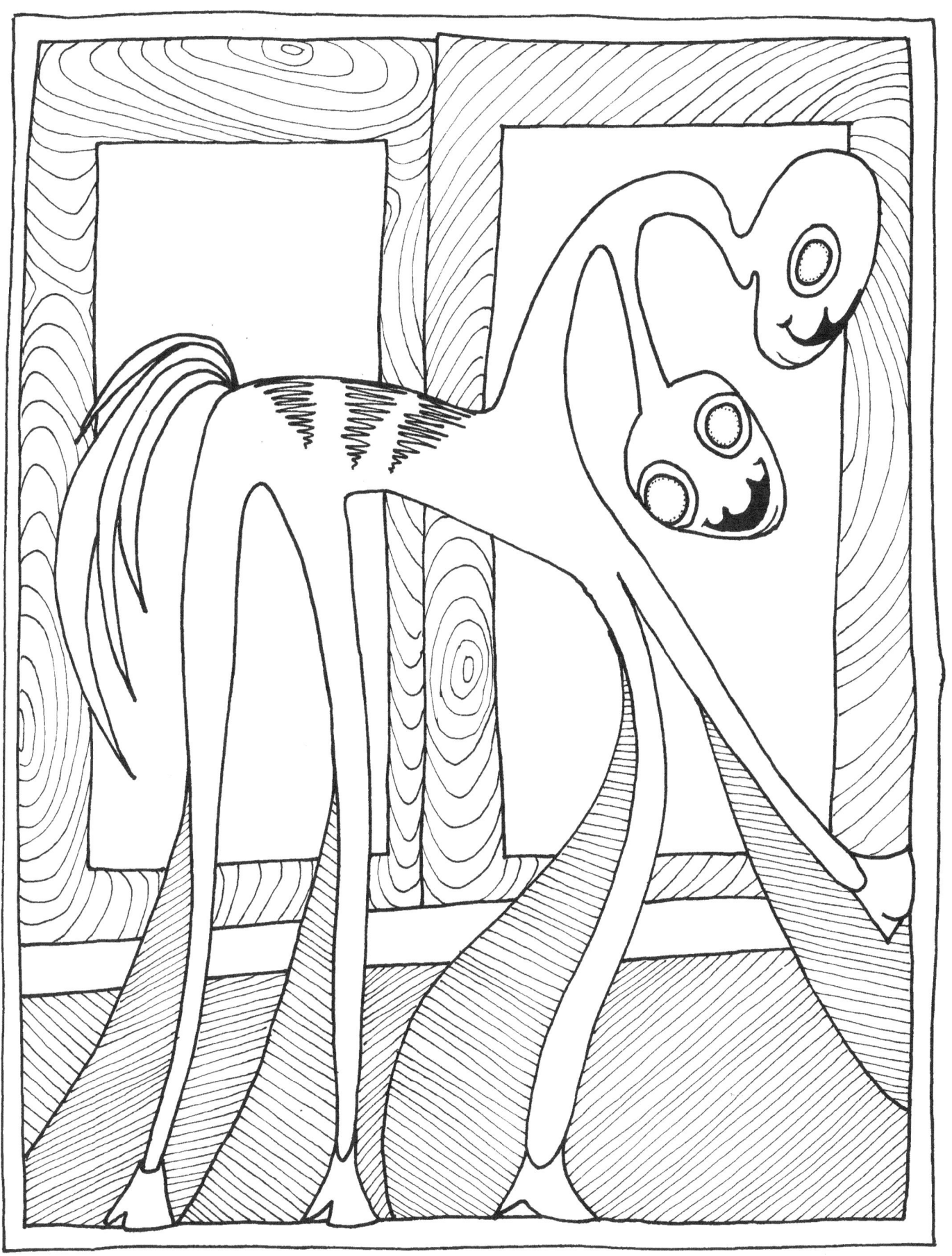

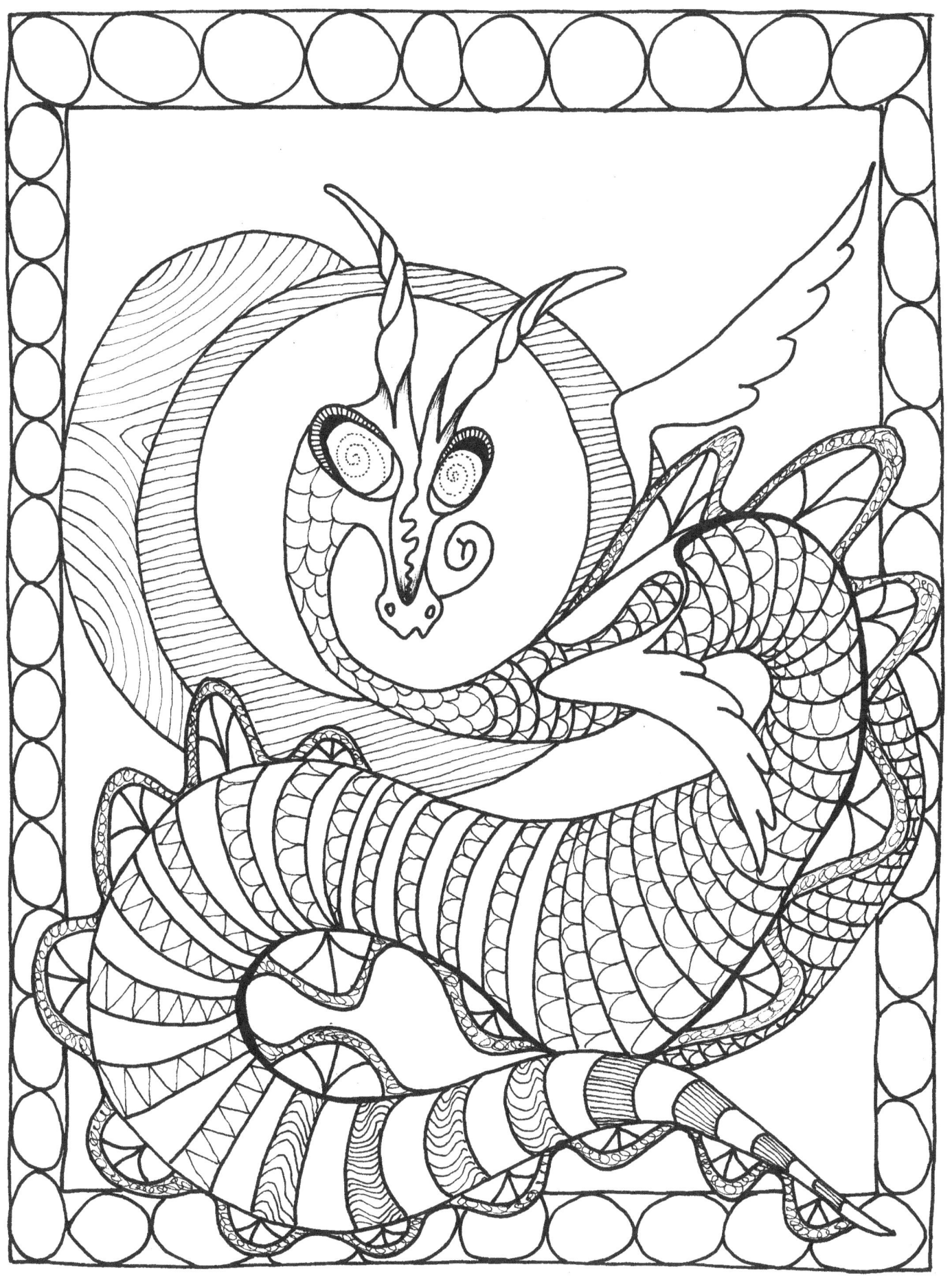

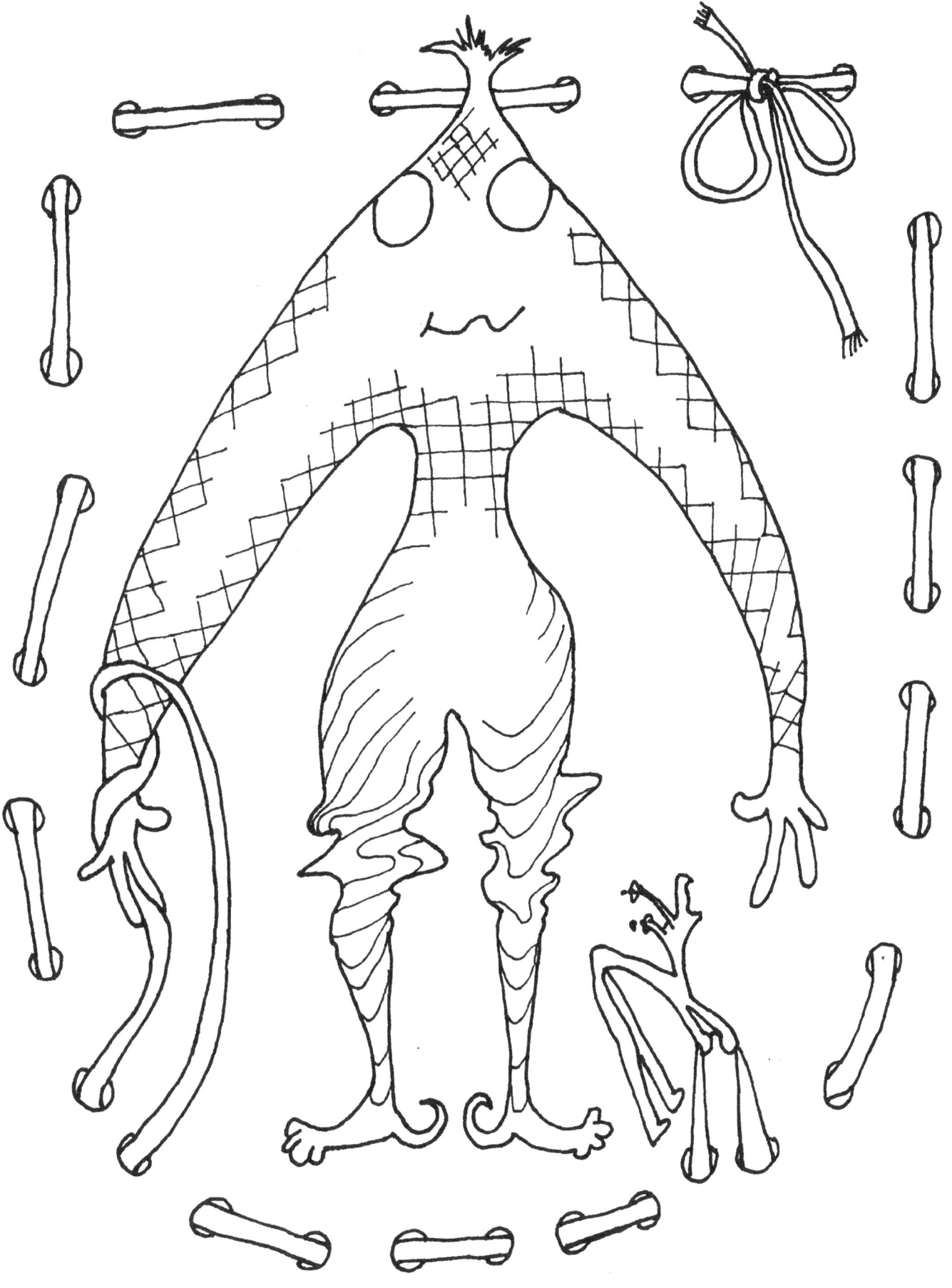

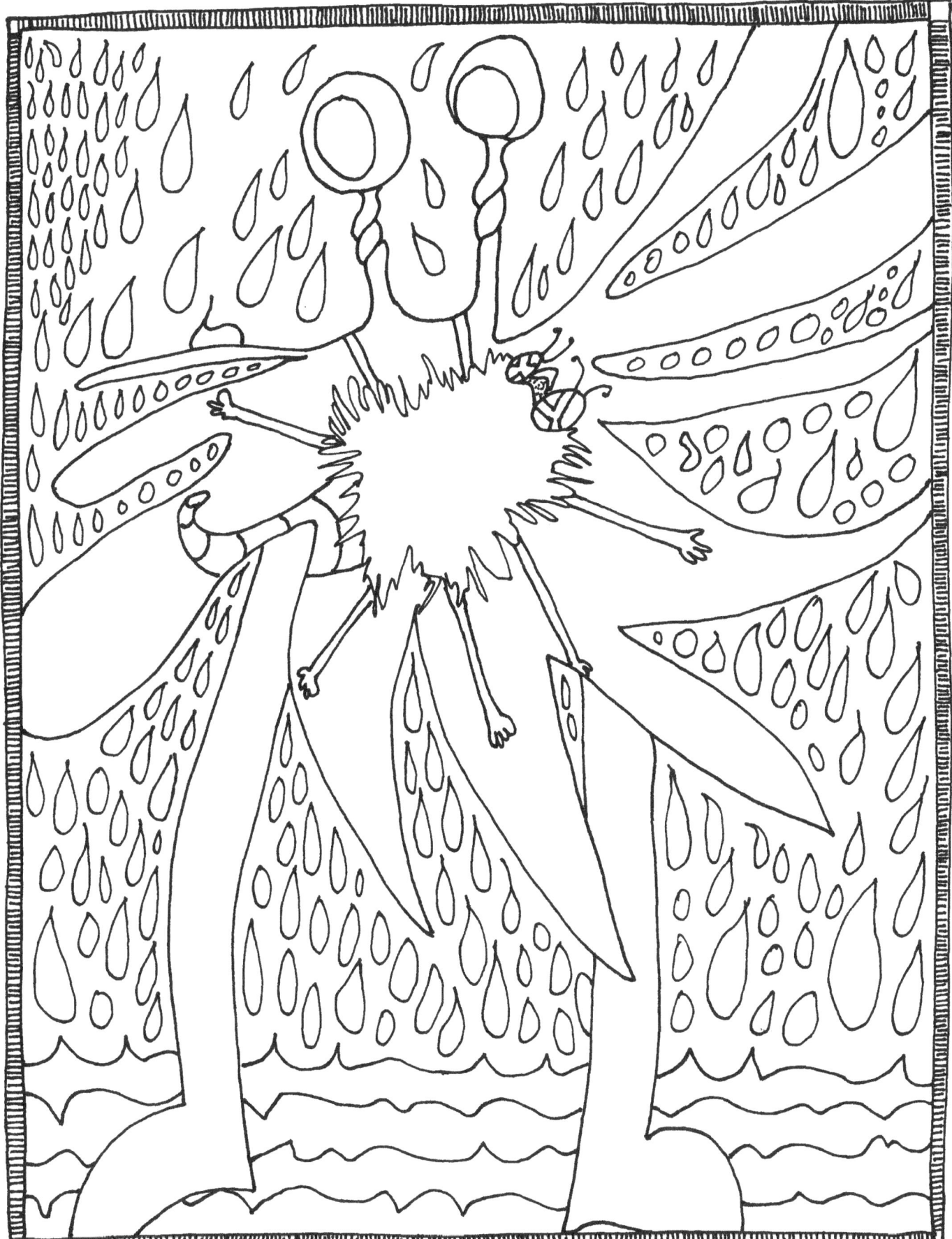

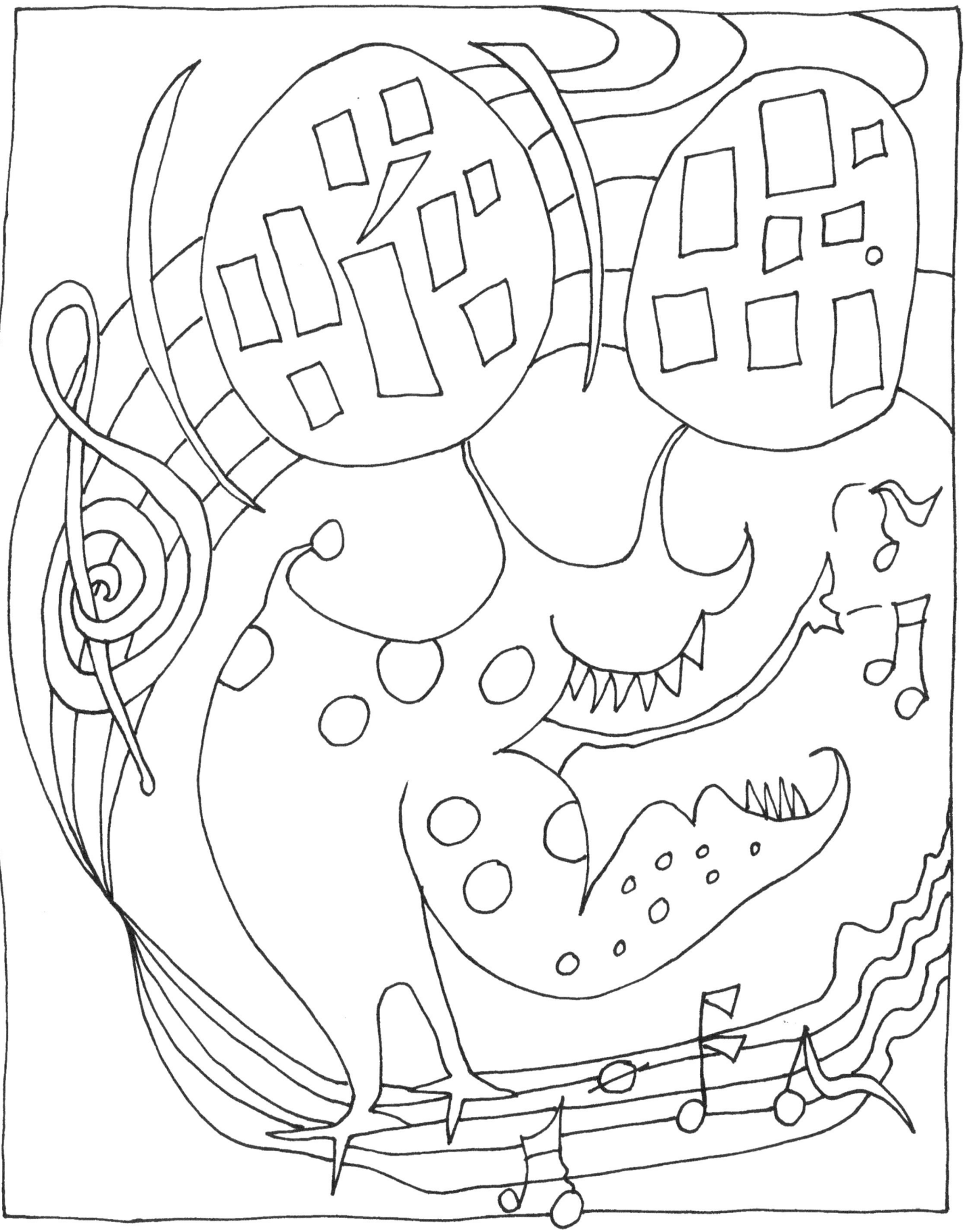

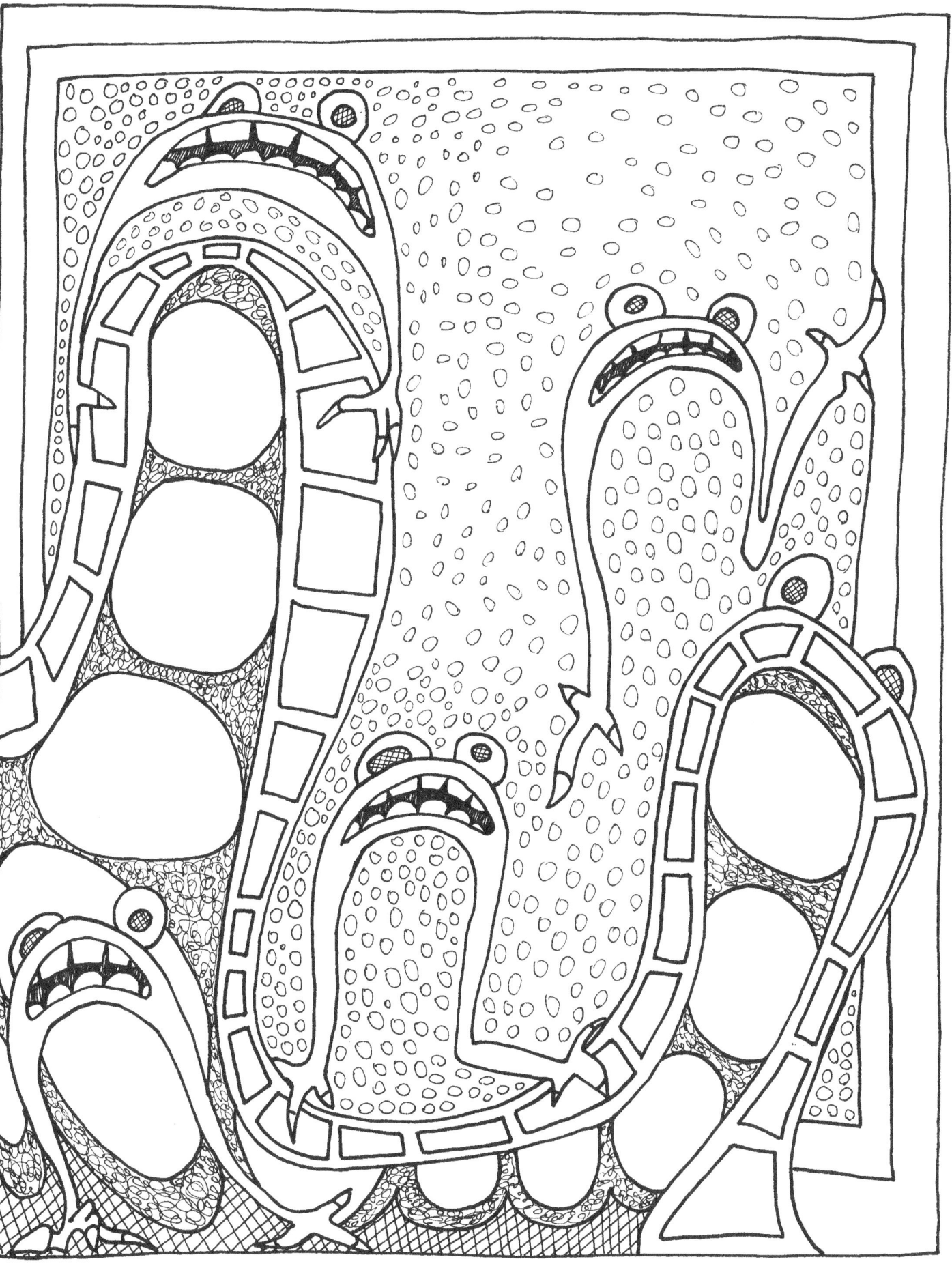

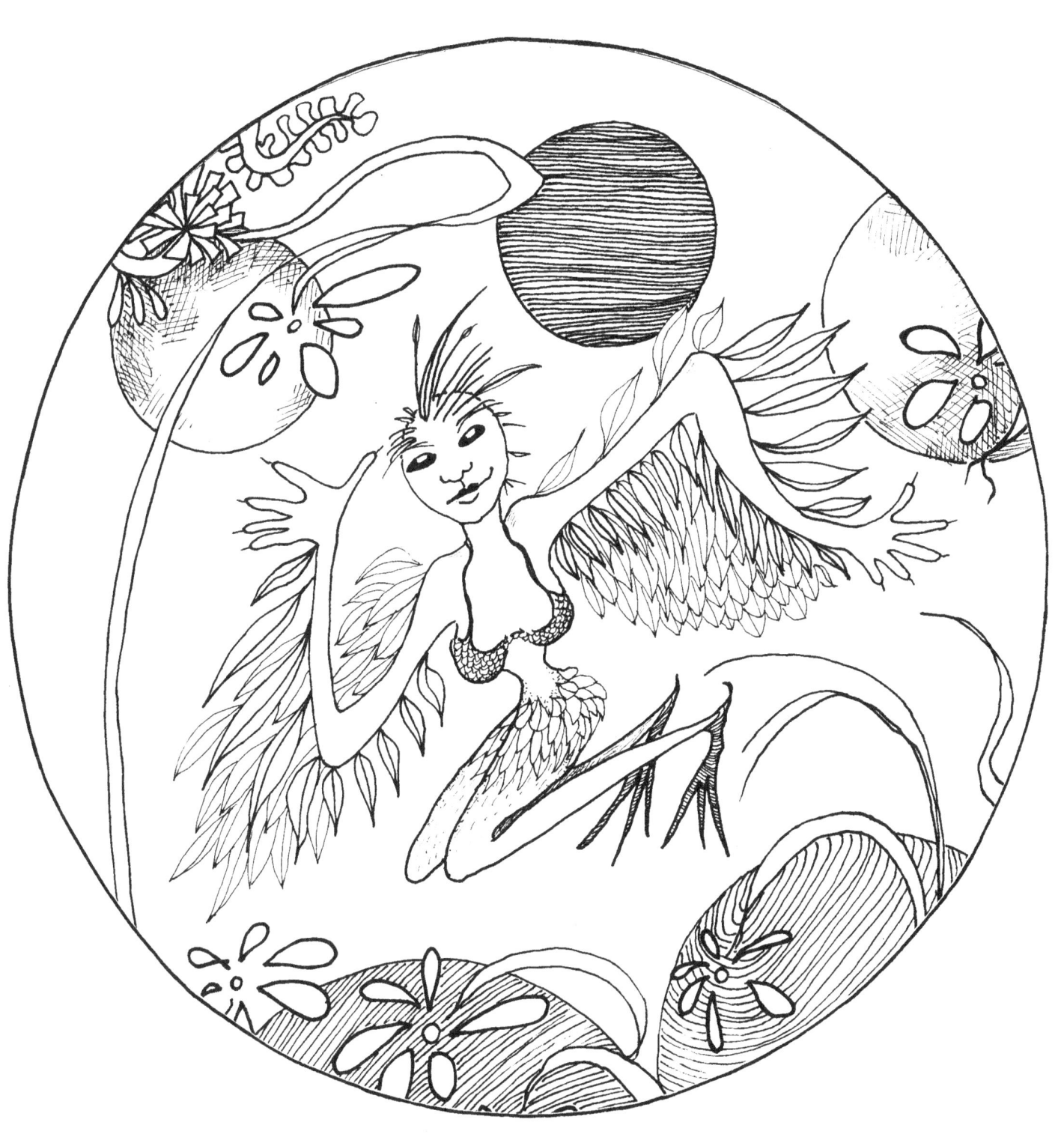

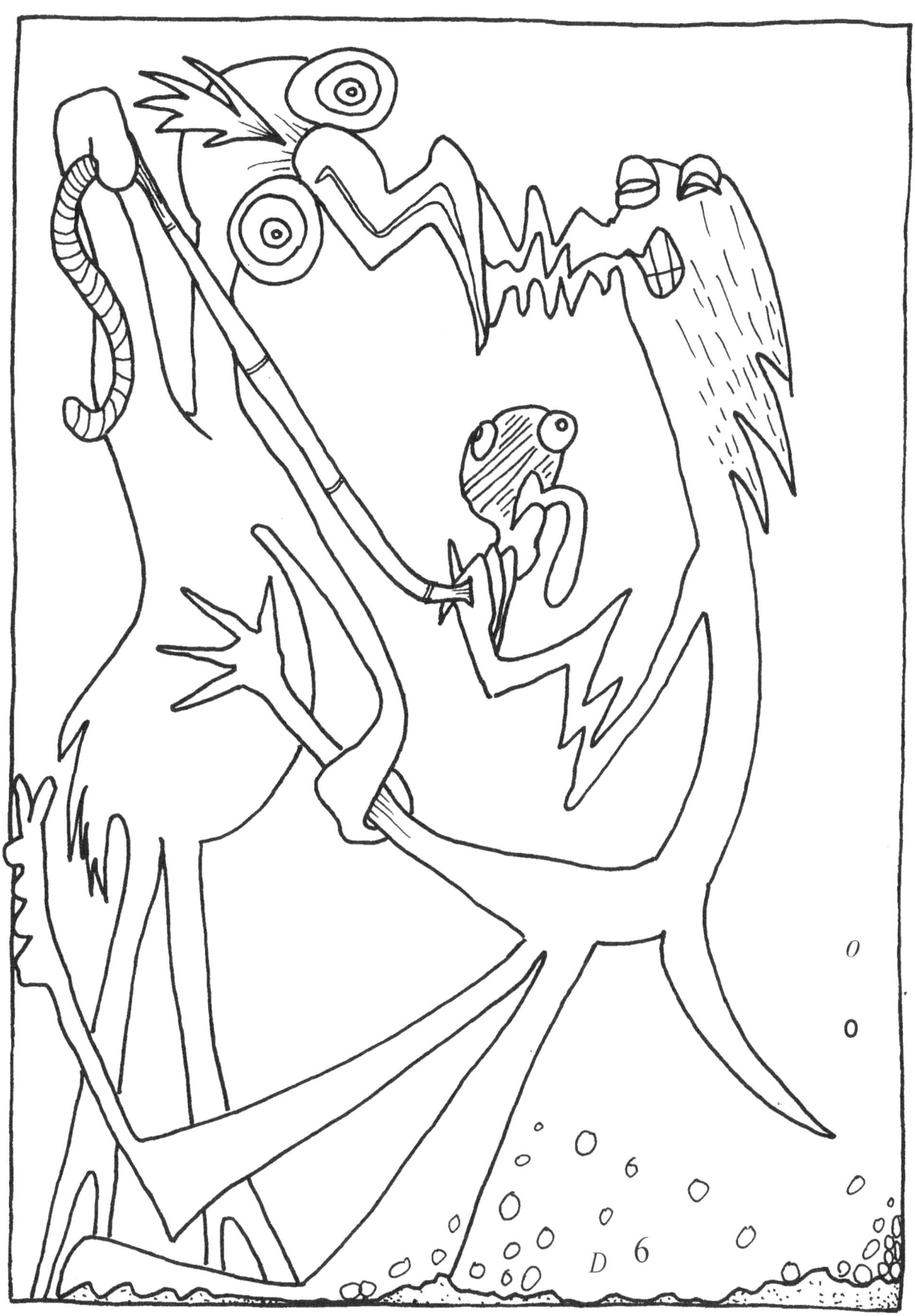

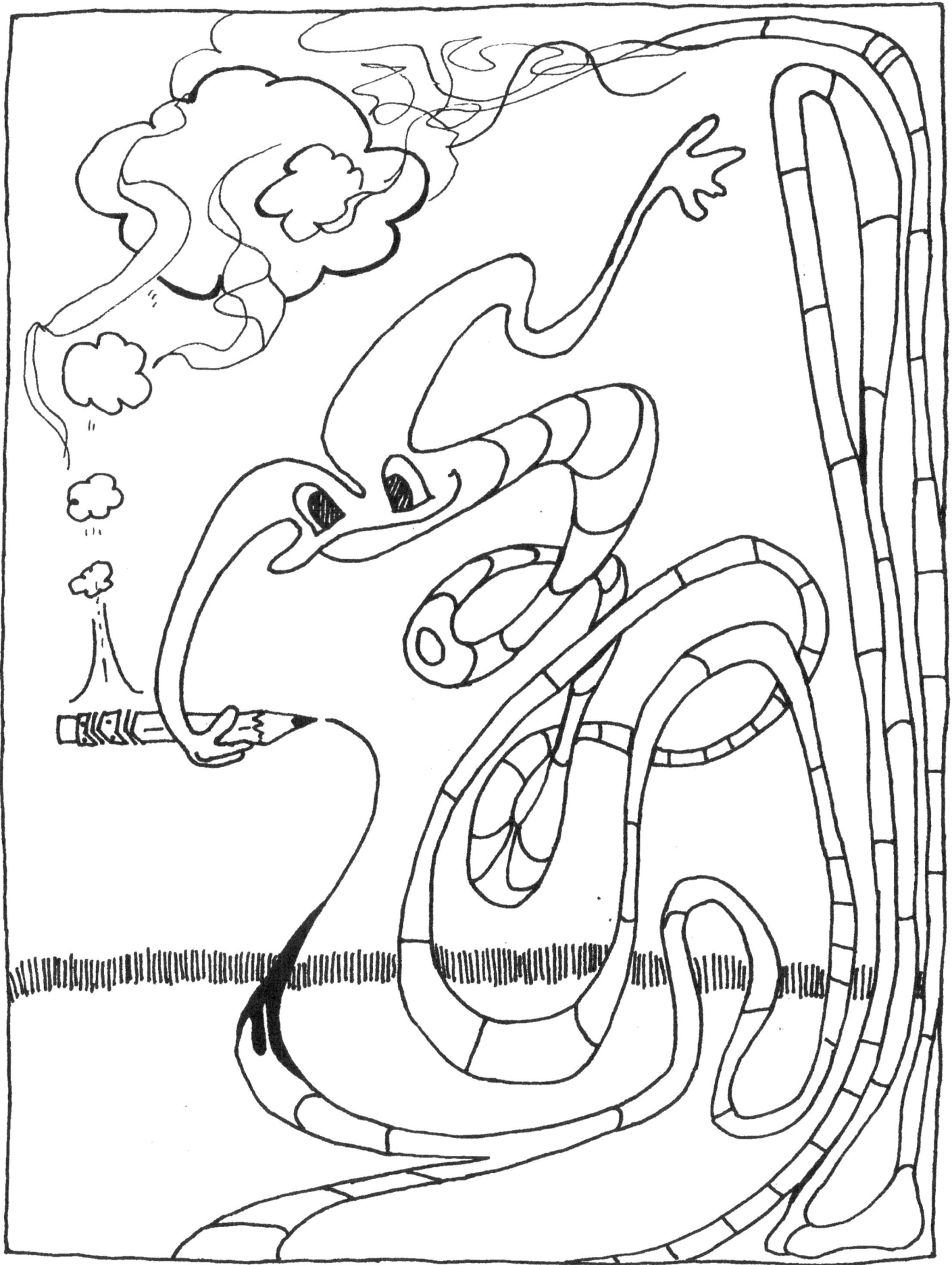

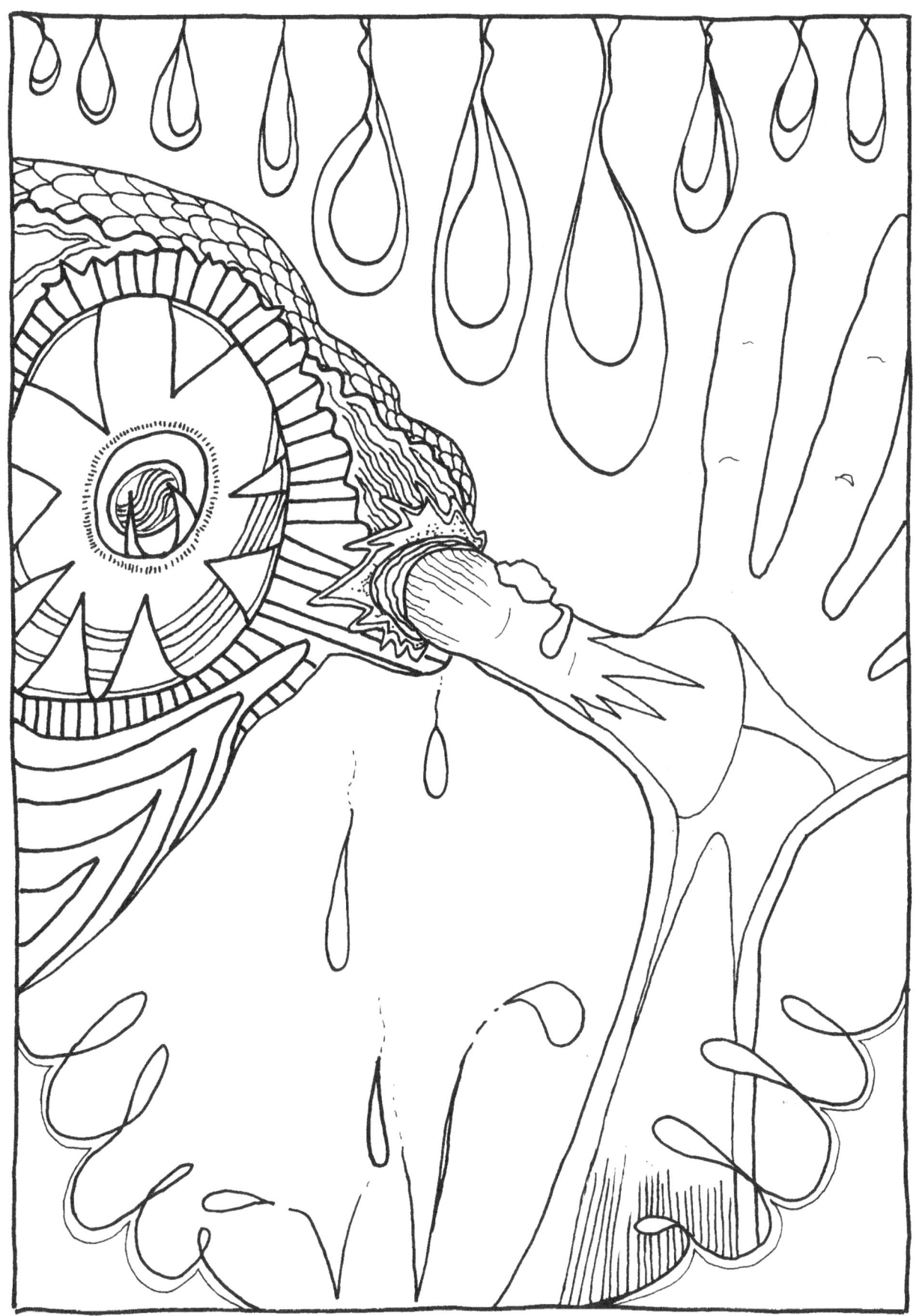

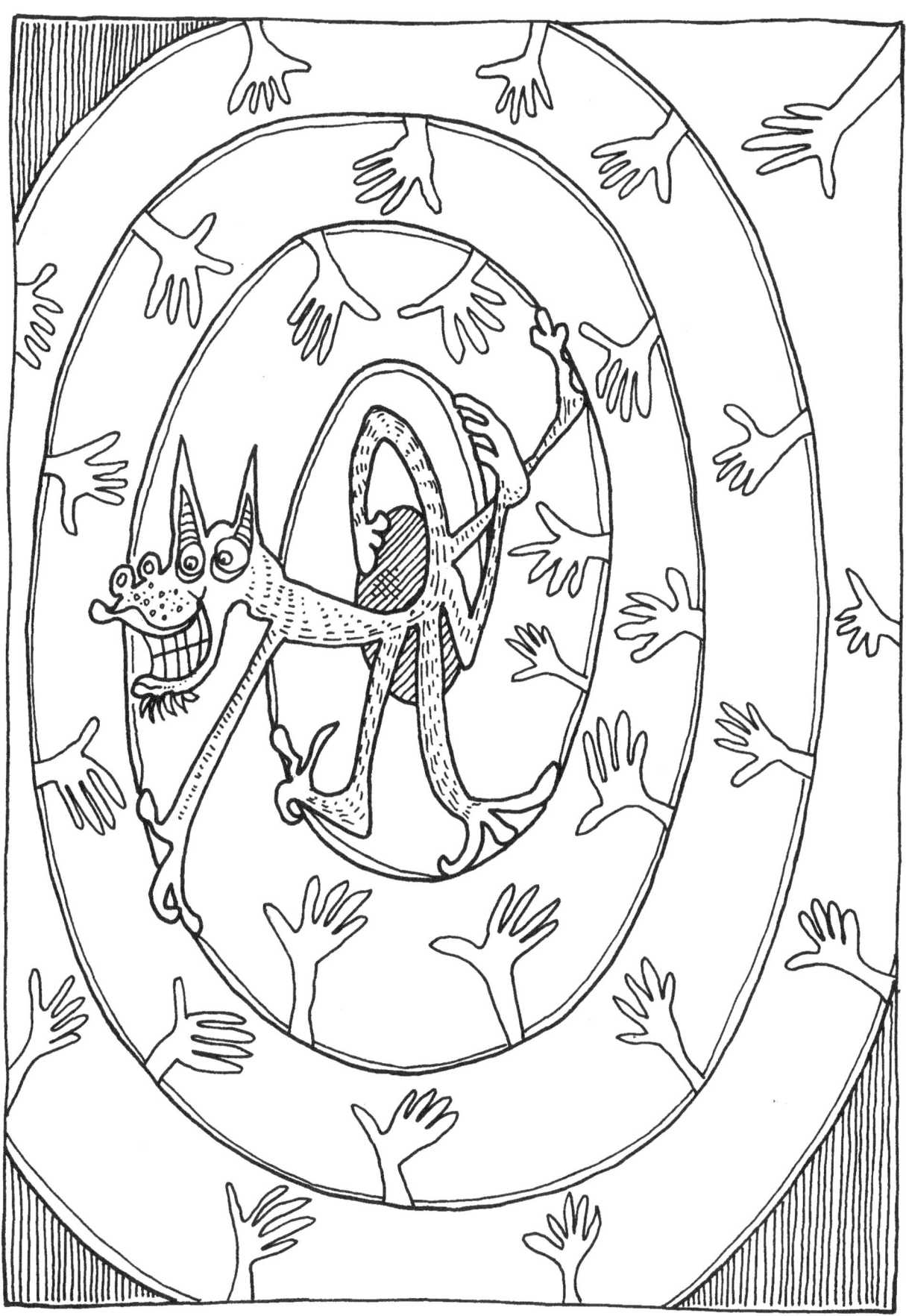

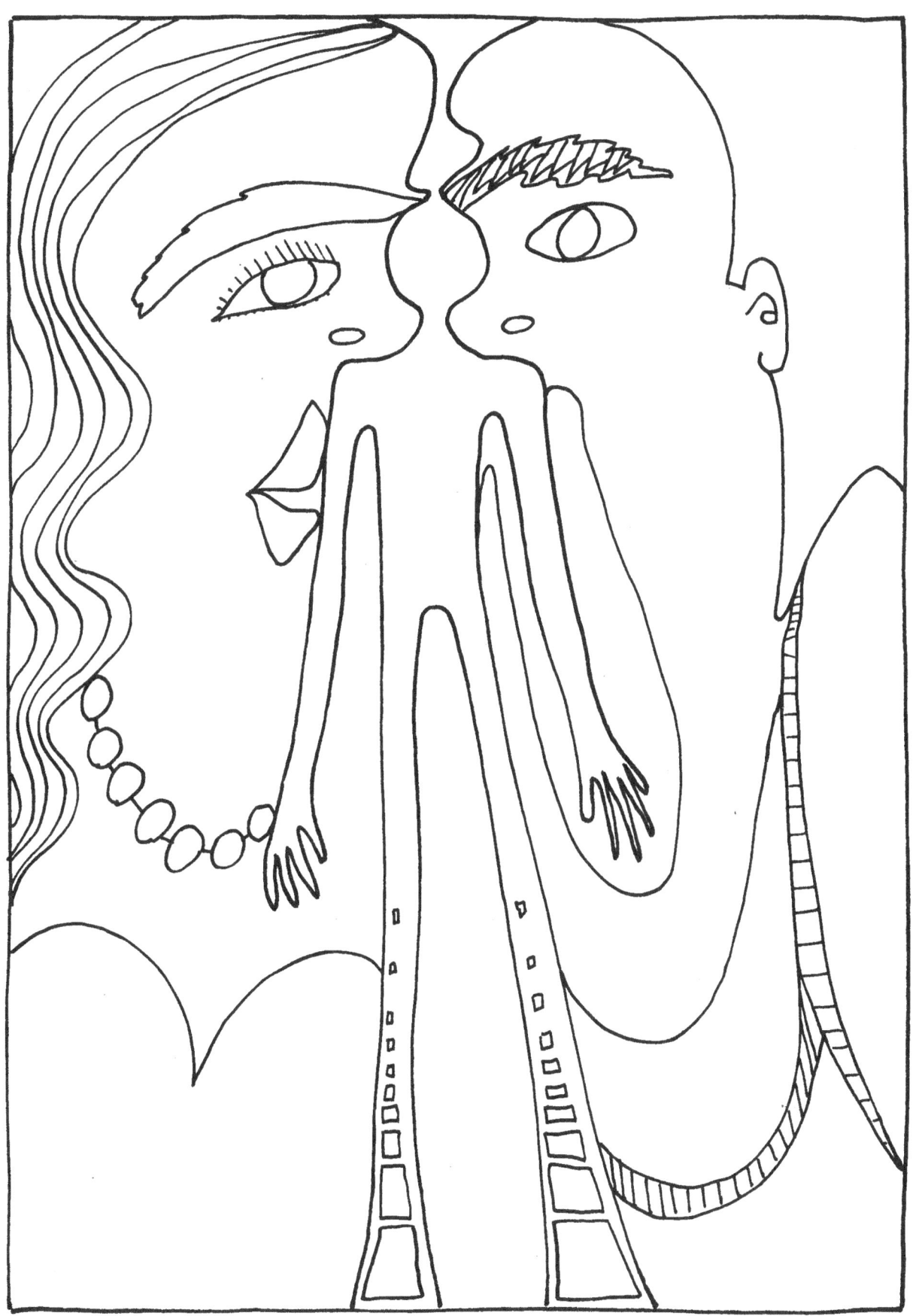

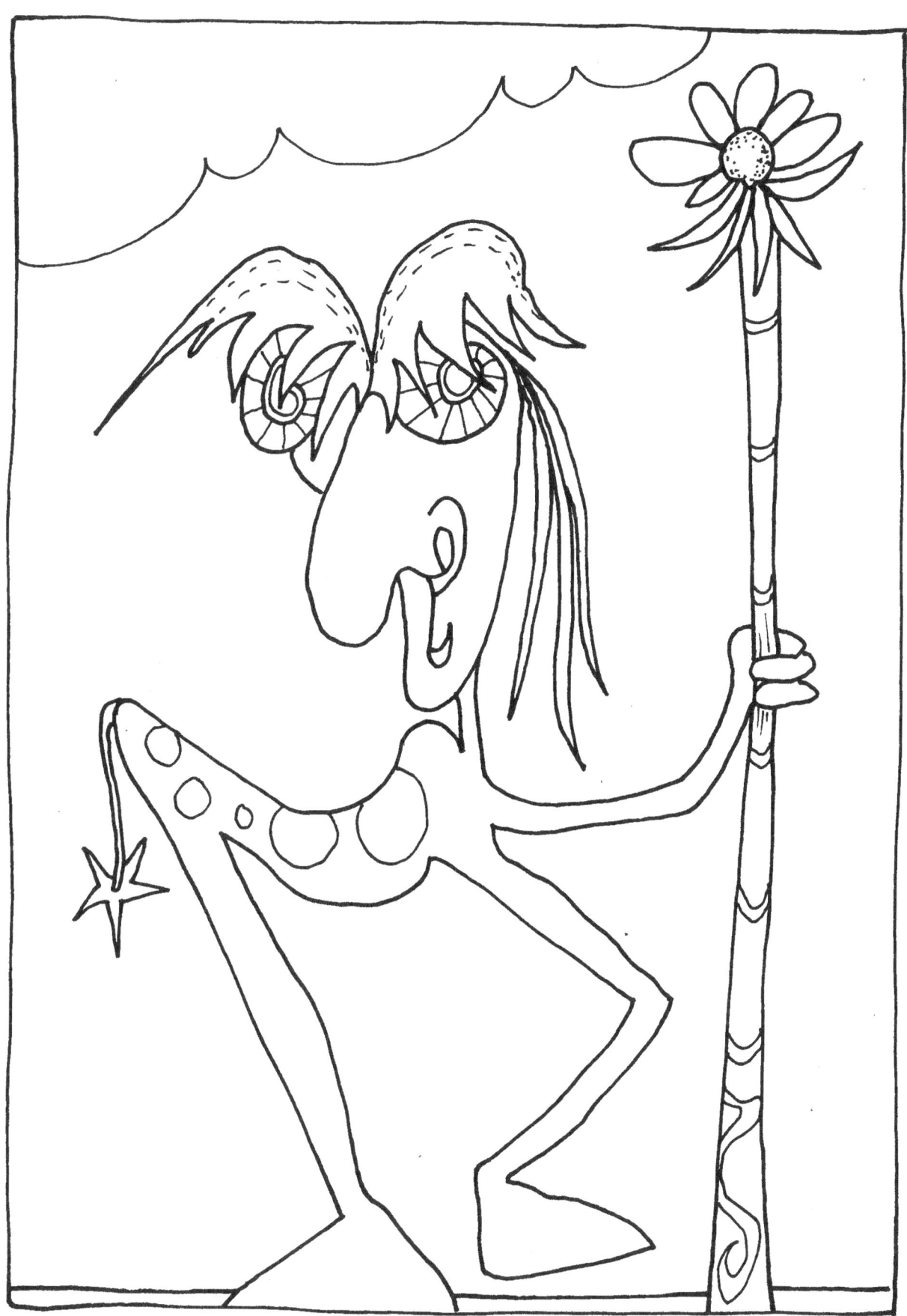

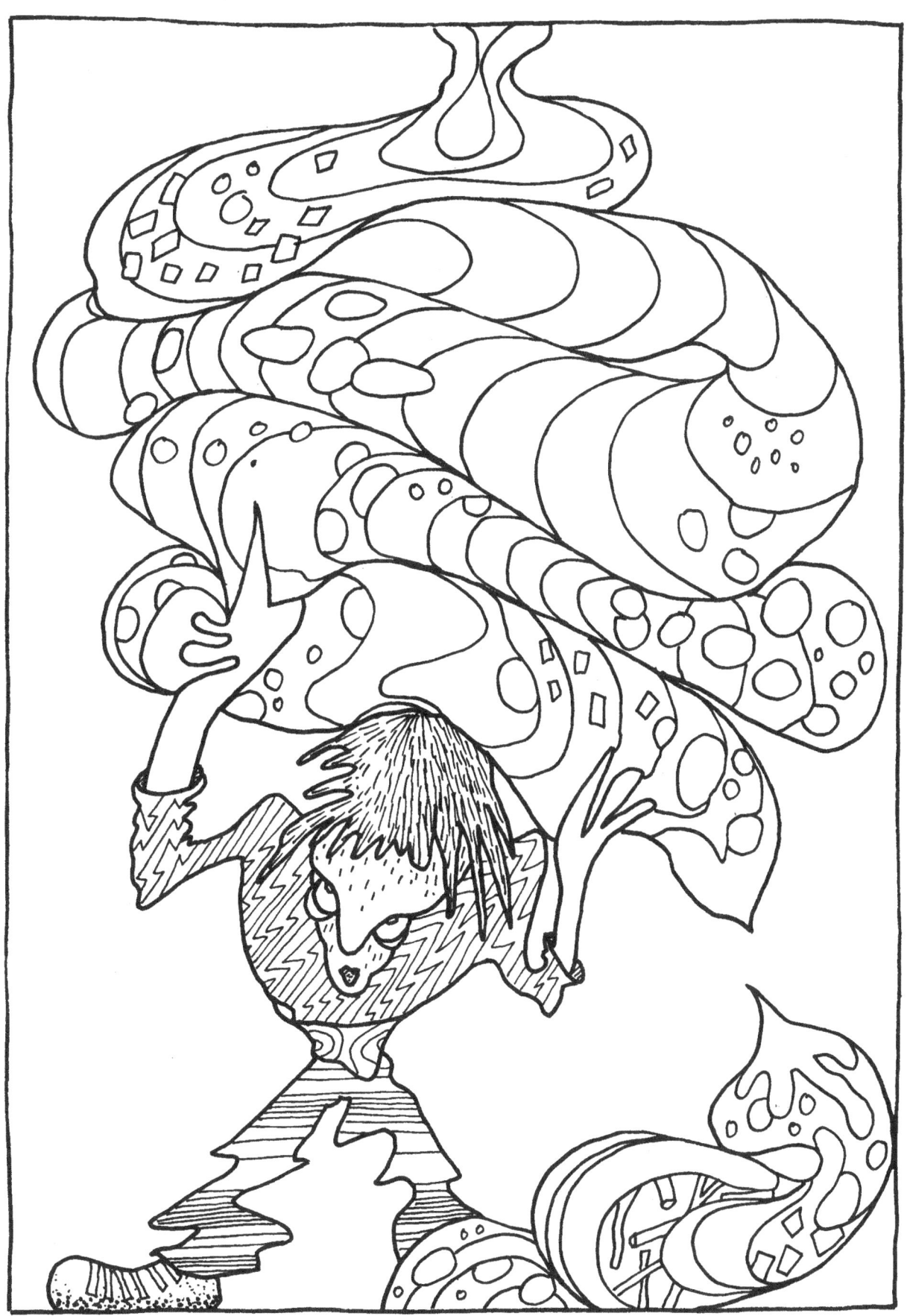

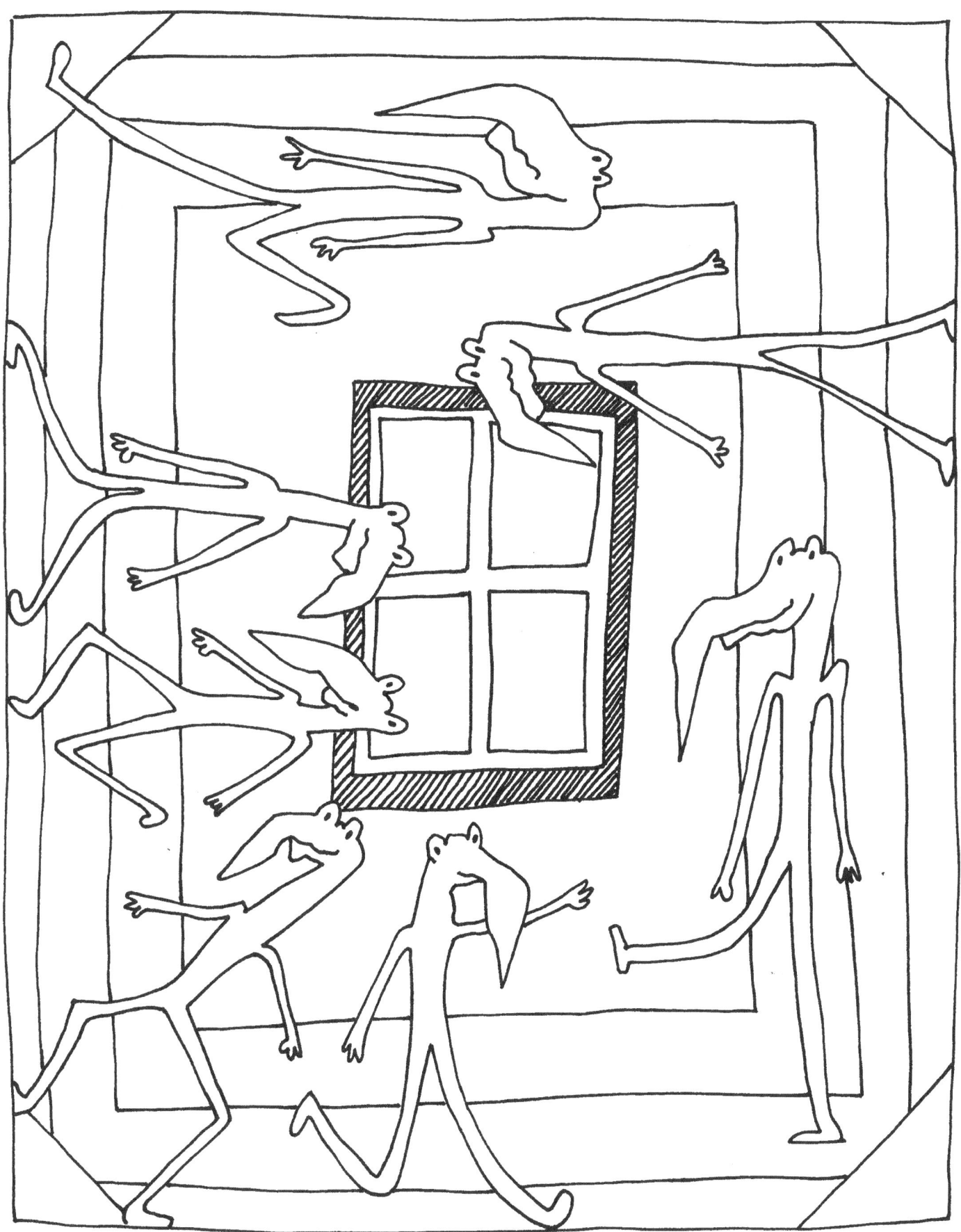

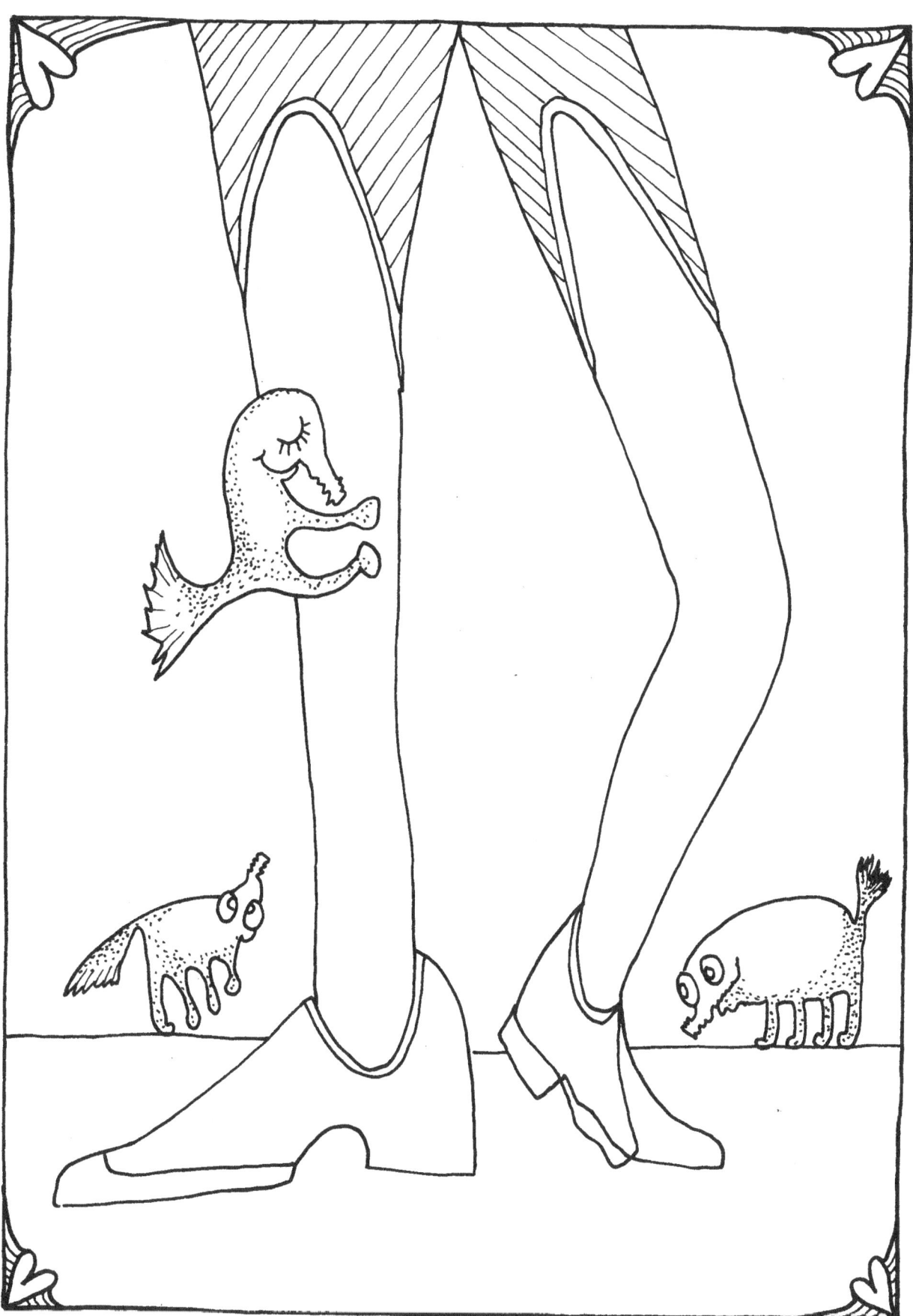

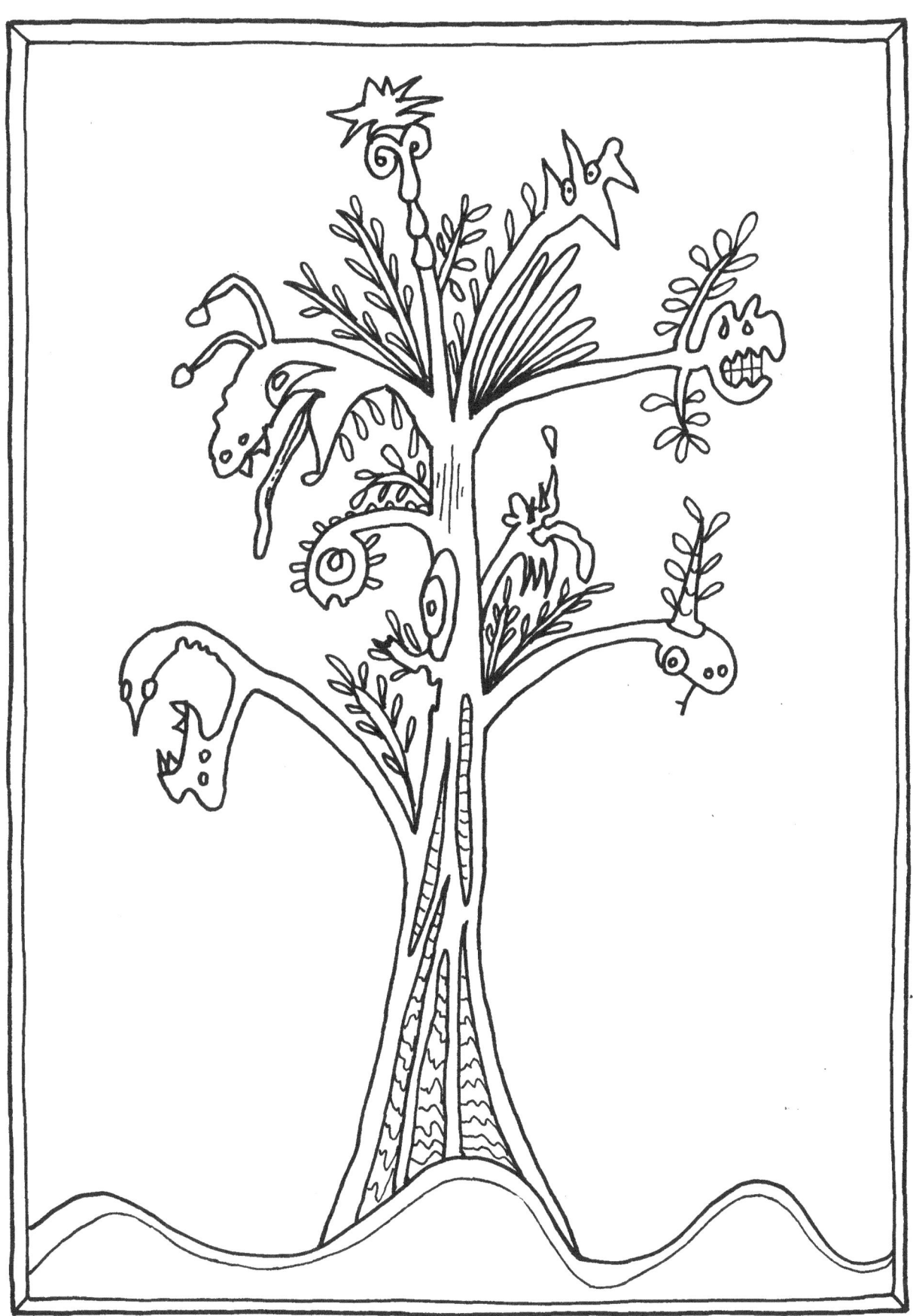

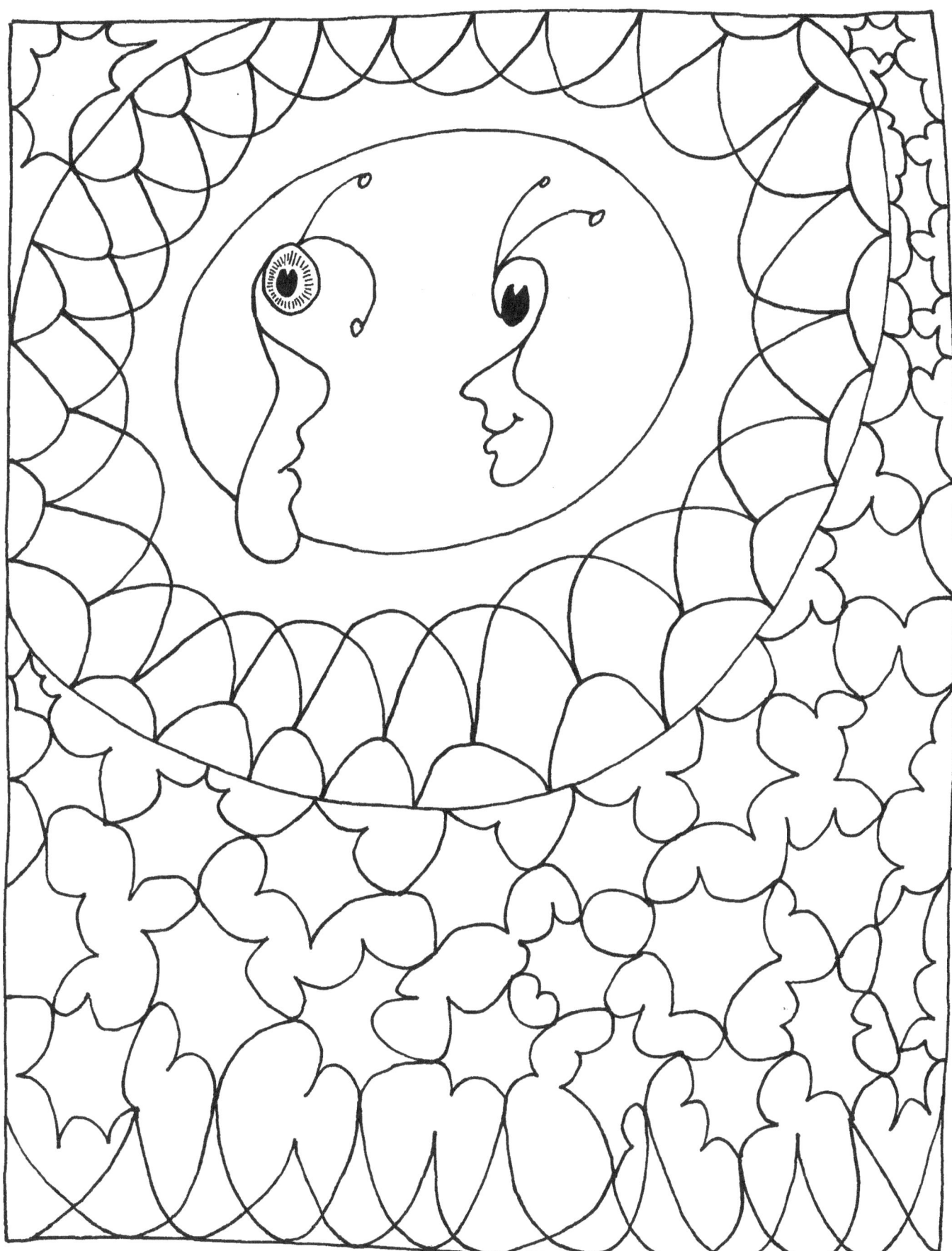

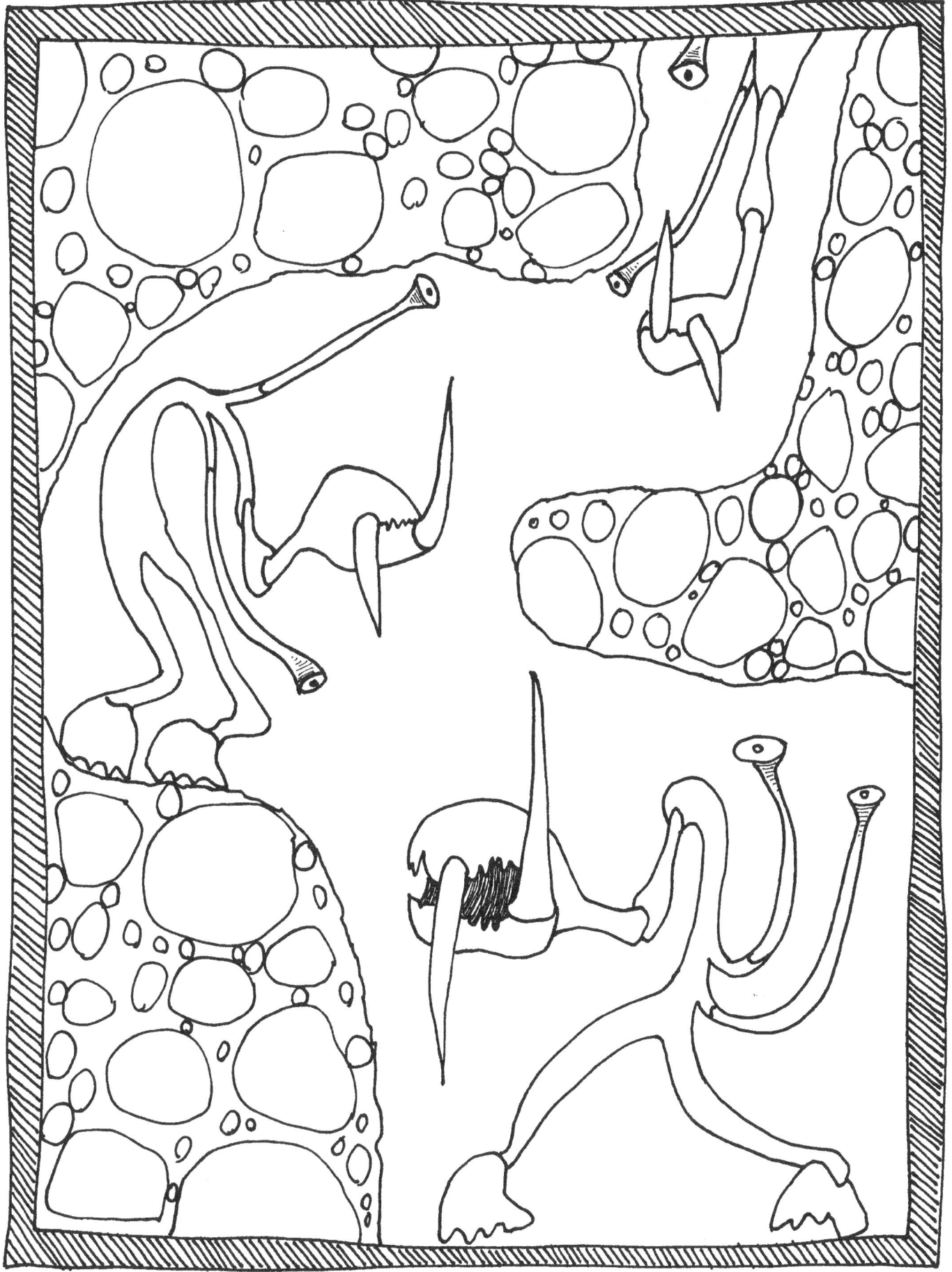

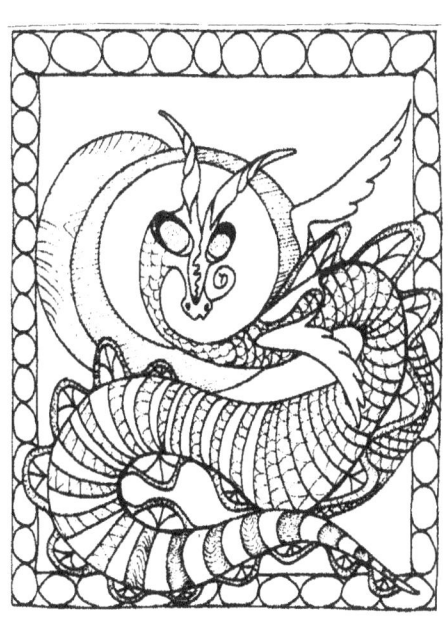

www.ingramcontent.com/pod-product-compliance
Lightning Source LLC
Chambersburg PA
CBHW081149180526
45170CB00006B/2001